JavaScript for Beginners: Unlocking the Power of Web Development

A Comprehensive Guide to Mastering JavaScript from Scratch

Alex Thompson

Table of Contents

INTRODUCTION

Welcome to "JavaScript for Beginners: Unlocking the Power of Web Development: A Comprehensive Guide to Mastering JavaScript from Scratch." This book is designed to be your gateway into the exciting world of JavaScript, the essential language that powers modern web development's dynamic and interactive aspects. Whether you're an absolute novice with no prior programming experience or someone with a basic understanding looking to deepen your knowledge, this guide will take you through the fundamentals and beyond.

JavaScript is more than just a programming language; it's a critical skill in today's digital landscape. As the backbone of web development, JavaScript enables you to create responsive, user-friendly websites and applications. This book breaks down complex concepts into manageable sections, ensuring you can follow along and build your confidence as you go.

Throughout these pages, you will set up your development environment, learn JavaScript's core syntax and features, and explore essential topics such as variables, functions, objects, and the Document Object Model (DOM). You will also delve into advanced topics like asynchronous programming and working with APIs. By the end of this book, you will understand how JavaScript works and be equipped with the skills to build your interactive projects.

Join us on this journey to unlock the power of web development with JavaScript. Let's embark on a path to mastery together, from the basics to becoming proficient in one of the most powerful tools in web development.

CHAPTER I

Say Hello To JavaScript

Welcome to JavaScript

Greetings from the realm of JavaScript, a vital tool that changed the web development process and continues to influence modern technology. Knowing JavaScript's significance, background, and development provides an essential context for understanding why it is still a mainstay of contemporary online development.

Programming languages like JavaScript let developers make dynamic and interactive web content. While HTML and CSS organize and style web pages, JavaScript adds functionality to improve the usability and engagement of websites. JavaScript has become an indispensable part of web development because it can be used to create interactive features like forms, animations, and real-time updates.

It is impossible to exaggerate the significance of JavaScript in contemporary web development. It forms the foundation of almost all web-based programs, ranging from straightforward web pages to intricate web apps. JavaScript is not limited to the front end; server-side programming is now possible with the introduction of environments such as Node.js. Because of its full-stack capability, developers can work on both the client and server sides using a single language, which expedites and improves development.

JavaScript's widespread ecosystem serves as another evidence of its prevalence. As frameworks and libraries like Angular, Vue.js, and React have grown in popularity, they provide pre-written code and other tools that make development easier and increase productivity. Built on top of JavaScript's basis, these frameworks and libraries increase its capability and facilitate the development of complex applications. Furthermore, JavaScript has a thriving developer community that supports and contributes to its ongoing development, keeping it current with the newest business practices and trends.

Understanding JavaScript's development and history is crucial to understanding its influence on web development. Brendan Eich developed JavaScript in 1995 while employed at Netscape Communications Corporation. The original objective was to create a scripting language capable of enhancing the interactivity of online pages. After being called Mocha, it was first renamed LiveScript and then JavaScript. Even though Java and JavaScript are fundamentally different programming languages, the term JavaScript was chosen as part of a marketing campaign to leverage the popularity of Java, another programming language at the time.

In approximately ten days, the first iteration of JavaScript was created and deployed along with Netscape Navigator

2.0. JavaScript gained popularity fast despite its hurried development because it improved user engagement on webpages. Nevertheless, the programming experience was fragmented due to the restricted capability and inconsistent behavior of early JavaScript versions across various web browsers.

The European Computer Manufacturers Association (ECMA) standardized JavaScript to respond to these difficulties. The first edition of ECMAScript, which was released in 1997, is the standardized version of JavaScript that is the product of this endeavor. The rise of JavaScript was greatly aided by this standardization, which gave browser vendors a uniform specification to follow, minimizing incompatibilities and enhancing the entire development environment.

Later iterations of ECMAScript carried on the development of JavaScript. A significant turning point was the 1999 introduction of ECMAScript 3, which included several crucial capabilities still in use today. However, conflicts about the direction of the language within the community led to the abandonment of ECMAScript 4, the next major version, after it encountered many difficulties.

When ECMAScript 5 was introduced in 2009, JavaScript underwent a sea change. Essential improvements, including strict mode, JSON support, and improved object properties, were included in this version, strengthening and simplifying the debugging of JavaScript. The next ten years would see fast developments in ECMAScript, primarily because of ECMAScript 5.

For JavaScript, a new era began in 2015 with the ECMAScript 6 (ES6) release. Significant improvements were brought about by ES6, including destructuring assignments, classes, modules, arrow functions, and template literals. With the addition of these features, the language became more expressive and more in line with other modern programming languages. The Promises notion, which is essential for managing asynchronous processes and is critical to contemporary online applications, was also introduced by ES6.

With the release of ES6, JavaScript continued to evolve. Every year, the ECMAScript specification is updated, bringing new capabilities and enhancements to the language. Async/await syntax makes writing and understanding asynchronous code more straightforward, and additional data structures like Map and Set, which expand the language's functionality, have been included in later versions.

The necessity to satisfy the requirements of more intricate online applications and consumers' rising expectations for rich, interactive experiences has fueled JavaScript's development. This progression demonstrates JavaScript's flexibility and durability, guaranteeing its continued use in the dynamic field of web development.

Apart from technological progress, the JavaScript ecosystem has experienced rapid expansion. Libraries and frameworks have been essential to this expansion. React, a Facebook product, introduced the notion of component-based architecture and completely changed the way developers create user experiences. While Vue.js offers a simple progressive framework to integrate into existing projects, Google's Angular provides a complete framework for building dynamic web apps. With these technologies, developers can now more efficiently and effectively design complex apps.

The influence of JavaScript goes beyond standard web browsers. JavaScript may now be used for server-side development, thanks to the popularity of Node.js, allowing programmers to create scalable network applications. Node.js is perfect for data-intensive applications because it makes use of JavaScript's event-driven, non-blocking I/O paradigm. JavaScript's status as a full-stack language that can handle both client-side and server-side development has been solidified by its adaptability.

In conclusion, there is no denying JavaScript's significance in contemporary web development. The web has changed, becoming more interesting and user-friendly thanks to its capacity to provide dynamic and interactive information. Its evolution and history highlight the language's durability and adaptability, guaranteeing its continuous relevance in the rapidly evolving digital ecosystem. JavaScript will continue to be a fundamental component of web development, enabling programmers to create inventive and engaging online experiences even as it develops. Acquiring proficiency in JavaScript is crucial for realizing the complete possibilities of web programming, regardless of experience level—greetings and welcome to JavaScript, the language behind the web.

Setting Up Your Environment

The first essential step for anyone starting with JavaScript web development is setting up a development environment. An efficient workspace can significantly increase output, optimize processes, and facilitate debugging. This procedure entails choosing and configuring a code editor and installing developer tools on a web browser. In this section , we'll go over how to install and set up the Chrome Developer Tools for the best possible work environment and how to use well-known code editors like Visual Studio Code (VS Code) and Sublime Text.

Web developers love Visual Studio Code, or VS Code, for its feature-rich feature set, ease of use, and versatility. It is one of the most widely used code editors. Before installing VS Code, visit the official Visual Studio Code website to obtain the installer appropriate for your operating system, be it Windows, macOS, or Linux. It's simple to install: launch the installer you downloaded and follow the prompts on the screen. After installation, you may open VS Code and start customizing it to your needs as a developer.

The extensibility of Visual Studio Code, exemplified by the multitude of extensions offered in the Visual Studio Code Marketplace, is one of its primary advantages. These addons improve productivity and offer functionality. A few extensions are very strongly advised for JavaScript development. The ESLint plugin provides real-time syntax and style issue highlighting, which aids in preserving code quality. Prettier is an extension that automatically formats your code based on pre-established principles, ensuring consistency throughout your project. Moreover, you may start a local development server with live reload capabilities using the Live Server extension, making observing changes as you write code more straightforward.

Setting up VS Code configuration entails personalizing settings to suit your needs by clicking on the gear icon in the bottom left of the window and choosing "Settings" from the menu. This is where you change the editor's theme, font size, and key bindings, among other things. Customizing the integrated terminal might also help you to improve workflow efficiency. You can configure the terminal to launch in the directory of your project and use the shell of your choice, such as Command Prompt, PowerShell, or Bash.

Another well-liked code editor that is renowned for its simplicity and quickness is Sublime Text. Visiting the Sublime Text website, downloading the installer for your operating system, and following the installation guidelines are the steps involved in installing Sublime Text. Sublime Text may be launched and configured for JavaScript development as soon as it is installed.

The Package Control extension can be used to control Sublime Text's package ecology, which is its power source. Press Ctrl+~ (backtick) to enter the Sublime Text console, then paste the installation command from the Package Control website to install Package Control. After installation, type "Install Package" into Ctrl+Shift+P to open Package Control. You can install different packages from here to improve your development environment. The Sublime Linter and Sublime Linter-eslint packages give real-time linting capabilities for JavaScript development, while the Babel package offers syntax highlighting for ES6 and React.

You can change Sublime Text's configuration by going to Preferences > Settings and changing the user preferences file. This is where you may change several options, including the indentation rules, theme, and font size. You may also establish project-specific parameters by storing your project files with a.sublime-project extension and defining project-specific settings within them. With this method, you can adjust the editor's behavior to suit the particular requirements of any project.

Setting up a web browser is as important as configuring a code editor for development purposes. Developers use Google Chrome because of its robust Developer Tools, which offer a range of functionalities for examining and troubleshooting web pages. Open Chrome and go to any webpage to get the Chrome Developer Tools. To access the Developer Tools panel, right-click the page, choose "Inspect" from the context menu, or use the keyboard shortcut Ctrl+Shift+I (or Cmd+Option+I on macOS).

The Chrome Developer Tools' Elements tab lets you view and work with a page's DOM and CSS. Elements in the HTML structure can be clicked to view the corresponding styles and make real-time modifications. Without changing your source code, this function is beneficial for troubleshooting layout problems and experimenting with different style modifications.

Another essential feature is the Console panel, which offers a command-line interface to interact with the JavaScript executing on the page. You may view error messages, log messages, and run JavaScript commands. This panel is a godsend for debugging JavaScript code because it lets you test code snippets and identify problems in the browser.

The Sources panel provides a complete interface for debugging JavaScript code. This is where you go through your code line by line, set breakpoints, and inspect and navigate your source files. To comprehend the execution flow and spot problems in your code, the panel also has tools like call stack examination and scope variable viewing.

The Network panel comes in handy when tracking and troubleshooting network requests. It offers comprehensive details about every request the page makes, including headers, response bodies, and timing information. This panel is convenient for troubleshooting API calls and ensuring your website loads resources quickly.

Tools for monitoring and controlling different web application components, such as local storage, session storage, cookies, and service workers, are available under the Application panel. Debugging problems with offline functionality and data durability requires using this panel. Chrome has several add-ons that work well with Developer Tools to improve your development workflow further. For instance, the Redux DevTools extension offers comparable capability for applications utilizing the Redux state management package. In contrast, the React Developer Tools extension gives further inspection and debugging tools for React applications.

In conclusion, correctly choosing and configuring a code editor and a web browser with developer tools are essential to setting up your working environment. Whichever editor you select—Sublime Text or Visual Studio Code—both provide a wealth of capabilities and allow for plugin and extension extensibility. Adapting these editors to your tastes and workflow will significantly increase productivity. Furthermore, installing Chrome Developer Tools gives you access to solid tools for testing, debugging, and optimizing your web apps. You may create the groundwork for a more productive and successful web development experience by setting up and configuring your development environment.

Writing Your First JavaScript Program

Writing your first JavaScript program marks an exciting step in your journey as a web developer. Understanding JavaScript's basic syntax and structure is crucial for building interactive web applications. This section will guide you through writing a simple JavaScript program, covering fundamental syntax and structure, and running JavaScript in the browser console to see the results of your code.

JavaScript, often abbreviated as JS, is a versatile and powerful programming language primarily used to enhance web pages' interactivity. Before diving into writing your first program, it is essential to understand JavaScript's basic syntax and structure. JavaScript code is written in plain text and is typically embedded within HTML documents using the <script> tag or included in separate .js files that the HTML then references. The basic building blocks of JavaScript include variables, data types, operators, and control structures.

You must set up a simple HTML file to begin writing your first JavaScript program. Open your preferred text editor, create a new file, and save it with a .html extension.

This HTML file creates a simple webpage with a title and a heading. The <script> tag at the bottom references an external JavaScript file named script.js, which will contain our JavaScript code. Please create a new file in the same directory as your HTML file and name it script.js. This file will be where we write our first JavaScript program.

JavaScript syntax is designed to be easy to understand and write. The first concept to grasp is variables. Variables store data that can be referenced and manipulated throughout your program. In JavaScript, variables can be declared using var, let, or const. The var keyword is the oldest way of declaring variables and is function-scoped. However, let and const are preferred in modern JavaScript because they provide block-scoping. The let keyword allows you to declare variables that can be reassigned, while const is used for variables that should not be reassigned after their initial value is set.

In this example, we declare a variable named greeting using the let keyword and assign it the "Hello, World!". We also declare a constant named pi using the const keyword and assign it the value 3.14159.

Another fundamental concept in JavaScript is data types. JavaScript supports several data types: strings, numbers, booleans, null, undefined, and objects. Strings are sequences of characters enclosed in single or double quotes. Numbers can be integers or floating-point values. Booleans represent true or false values. Null is an exceptional value representing the absence of any value, while undefined is a value assigned to variables that have been declared but not initialized.

In this example, we declare variables with different data types: a string, a number, a boolean, a null value, and an undefined variable.

JavaScript also includes various operators for performing operations on variables and values. Common operators include arithmetic operators (+, -, *, /, %), comparison operators (==, ===, !=, !==, >, <, >=, <=), and logical operators (&&, ||, !).

Control structures are another crucial aspect of JavaScript. They allow you to control the flow of your program based on conditions. The most common control structures are if-else statements, switch statements, loops, while loops, and do-while loops.

In this example, the if-else statement checks whether the age variable is greater than or equal to 18 and prints a message accordingly. The for loop iterates five times, printing the iteration number each time.

Once you have written your JavaScript code in the script.js file, you can run it in the browser console to see the results. Open your web browser (Google Chrome is recommended) and navigate to your HTML file's directory. Open the HTML file in the browser to see your webpage. To access the browser console, right-click on the webpage and select "Inspect" or press Ctrl+Shift+I (Cmd+Option+I on macOS) to open the Developer Tools. Then, click on the "Console" tab to open the console.

You can see any messages or output from your JavaScript code in the console. If you followed the examples above, you should see the messages "You are an adult." and "Iteration 0" to "Iteration 4" printed in the console. The console is a powerful tool for testing and debugging your JavaScript code. You can also type JavaScript commands directly into the console and see the results immediately. For example, try typing console.log("Hello, Console!")

and press Enter to see the message printed in the console.

The browser console is not only helpful in viewing output but also for debugging errors. If your JavaScript code has syntax errors or issues, the console will display error messages about what went wrong and where the error occurred. This feedback is invaluable for identifying and fixing problems in your code.

In addition to the primary console, modern browsers provide enhanced debugging capabilities. For instance, Chrome Developer Tools offer features like setting breakpoints, stepping through code, and inspecting variables' values at different execution points. To set a breakpoint, open the "Sources" tab in Developer Tools, navigate to your script.js file, and click on the line number where you want to pause execution. When the code execution reaches that line, it will pause, allowing you to inspect the current state of your program.

Writing your first JavaScript program involves understanding basic syntax and structure, which includes variables, data types, operators, and control structures. You can begin experimenting with JavaScript code by creating a simple HTML file and linking it to a JavaScript file. Running your JavaScript code in the browser console allows you to see the output and debug any issues, making the development process interactive and engaging. As you become more comfortable with these fundamentals, you will be well-equipped to explore more advanced JavaScript concepts and build dynamic, interactive web applications.

CHAPTER II

JavaScript Basics

Understanding Variables and Data Types

Understanding variables and data types is fundamental to mastering JavaScript, as they form the backbone of how data is handled within the language. JavaScript uses variables to store information that can be manipulated and retrieved later, and it supports several types of variables and data types. Among the most critical concepts are the `var,` `let,` and `const` keywords for variable declaration and the primitive data types: string, number, boolean, null, undefined, and symbol. This section will explore these concepts in detail.

In JavaScript, variables are containers for storing data values. The keyword used to declare a variable determines its scope, reassign ability, and hoisting behavior. Traditionally, JavaScript only had the `var` keyword, function-scoped. This means that a variable declared with `var` is accessible anywhere within the function it was stated in. However, `var` has some drawbacks, particularly related to hoisting and its function scope, which can lead to unintended consequences.

Hoisting is a JavaScript behavior where variable and function declarations are moved to the top of their scope during compilation. With `var,` this can lead to confusing bugs because a variable can be referenced before declared, resulting in `undefined.`

To address some of these issues, ES6 (ECMAScript 2015) introduced two new keywords for variable declaration: `let` and `const.` Variables declared with `let` are block-scoped, meaning they are only accessible within the block they are declared in, such as within a loop or an if statement. This reduces the risk of variables being accessed or modified outside their intended scope.

The `const` keyword, like `let,` is also block-scoped but is used to declare variables that should not be reassigned. While the value of a `const` variable itself cannot be changed, if the variable points to an object or array, the contents of that object or array can still be modified.

Understanding these variable declarations is crucial for writing clear, maintainable code.

Moving on to data types, JavaScript has several primitive data types of fundamental to the language. These are `string,` `number,` `boolean,` `null,` `undefined,` and `symbol.` Primitive data types are immutable, meaning their values cannot be changed once created, although the variables that contain them can be reassigned.

Strings in JavaScript are used to represent text and are created by enclosing characters in single quotes ("`), double quotes (`" `), or backticks ("` "). Backticks, also known as template literals, allow for embedded expressions using `${}` and can span multiple lines.

Numbers in JavaScript represent both integer and floating-point values. JavaScript uses a single number type, unlike some languages that distinguish between integers and floats. Operations with numbers are straightforward, involving standard arithmetic operators like `+,` `-,` `*,` `/,` and `%. Booleans are simple data types with one of two values: `true` or `false.` They are commonly used in conditional statements to control the flow of a program.

The `null` data type is an exceptional value representing the intentional absence of any object value. It is often used to indicate that a variable should have no value.

`Undefined` is another particular data type. A variable declared but not initialized to any value will have the value `undefined.` This indicates that the variable exists but has not been assigned a specific value.

The `symbol` data type, introduced in ES6, is a unique and immutable primitive value often used to identify object properties uniquely. Symbols are created using the `Symbol` function. Each emblem is exceptional, even if they have the same description.

Symbols are handy in scenarios where property names must be unique to avoid name clashes, such as when creating libraries or frameworks.

In JavaScript, understanding how to use these primitive data types effectively is essential. They form the building blocks of the language, and much of JavaScript programming involves working with these types. Each type serves a specific purpose and has methods and properties that can be utilized.

For instance, strings come with a variety of methods for manipulation and querying, such as `.length` to get the string's length, `.to Uppercase()` to convert to uppercase, and `.slice()` to extract a part of the string.

Numbers have methods like `Math. Round ()`, `Math. Floor ()`, and `Math. Random ()`, which is helpful for mathematical operations. Booleans, though more straightforward, are critical in control structures to determine the execution flow of programs.

In conclusion, understanding variables and data types in JavaScript is fundamental to mastering the language. The `var,` `let,` and `const` keywords serve unique purposes in a variable declaration, offering different scoping rules and reassignment capabilities. Primitive data types—string, number, boolean, null, undefined, and symbol—are essential for storing and manipulating data. Grasping these concepts allows developers to write more effective and bug-free code, forming a solid foundation for further exploration into JavaScript's more advanced features.

Operators and Expressions

Understanding operators and expressions in JavaScript is crucial for performing computations, making decisions, and controlling the flow of your programs. Operators are symbols that perform operations on variables and values, and expressions combine variables, values, and operators to produce results. This section will delve into three primary categories of operators: arithmetic operators, comparison operators, and logical operators.

Arithmetic operators are fundamental in any programming language, and JavaScript is no exception. These operators perform basic mathematical operations on numbers. The primary arithmetic operators in JavaScript include addition (+), subtraction (-), multiplication (*), division (/), and modulus (%). These operators work as expected, performing the corresponding mathematical operation.

For example, the addition operator adds two numbers: javascript let sum = 5 + 3; // sum is 8. Similarly, subtraction subtracts the second number from the first:

Javascript let difference = 10 - 4; // difference is 6. Multiplication and division follow the same pattern:

Javascript let product = 6 x 7; // product is 42 let quotient = 20 / 5; // quotient is 4. The modulus operator returns the remainder of the division of two numbers:

Javascript let remainder = 10 % 3; // remainder is 1.

In addition to these basic arithmetic operators, JavaScript also supports increment (++) and decrement (--) operators, which increase or decrease a variable's value by one. These operators can be used in both prefix and postfix forms, with slightly different effects:

Javascript let x = 5; x++; // x is now 6 ++x; // x is now 7.

let y = 5; y--; // y is now 4 --y; // y is now 3.

Arithmetic operations are essential for tasks ranging from simple calculations to complex algorithms. Understanding how to use these operators effectively allows you to manipulate numerical data accurately and efficiently.

Comparison operators are another vital category, enabling you to compare values and determine relationships between them. Based on the comparison, these operators return a boolean value (true or false). The primary comparison operators include equal to (==), strictly equal to (===), not equal to (!=), strictly not equal to (!==), greater than (>), less than (<), greater than or equal to (>=), and less than or equal to (<=).

The equal to (==) operator checks if two values are equal, performing type coercion if necessary:

Javascript console.log(5 == '5'); // true

On the other hand, the strictly equal to (===) operator checks for both value and type equality: javascript

console. log(5 === '5'); // false

Similarly, the not equal to (!=) operator checks if two values are not equal, with type coercion: javascript console. log(5 != '5'); // false

The strictly not equal to (!==) operator checks for value and type inequality: javascript: console. log(5 !== '5'); // true The greater than (>) and less than (<) operators compare the relative size of two values: javascript: console.log(7 > 5); //actual: console.log(3 < 8); //actual.

Greater than or equal to (>=) and less than or equal to (<=) operators check for inequality, including equality: javascript: console. log(7 >= 7); // true: console. log(5 <= 5); // true.

These comparison operators are crucial for controlling the flow of your programs, particularly within conditional statements and loops. They allow you to make decisions based on dynamic conditions, enhancing the interactivity and complexity of your applications.

Logical operators, the third category, combine multiple boolean expressions and return a boolean result. The primary logical operators in JavaScript are logical AND (&&), logical OR (||), and logical NOT (!).

The logical AND (&&) operator returns true if both operands are valid; otherwise, it returns false. This operator is often used to ensure that multiple conditions are met: javascript

let age = 25; let has License = true, if (age > 18 && has license) { console. log('You can drive.');}

In this example, the message will be logged only if both conditions (age greater than 18 and having a license) are accurate.

The logical OR (||) operator returns true if at least one of the operands is true; otherwise, it returns false. This operator is useful for checking if at least one of multiple conditions is met: javascript: let weekend = true; let is Holiday = false.

If (weekend || holiday) {console.log('You can relax.');}

In this example, the message will be logged if it is either the weekend, a holiday, or both.

The logical NOT (!) operator inverts the boolean value of its operand. If the operand is true, the result will be false, and vice versa. This operator is often used to toggle boolean values or to ensure a condition is not met: javascript:

let is Raining = false; if (!is Raining) {console.log('You can go outside.');}```

In this example, the message will be logged if it is not raining.

Combining logical operators allows for complex conditional logic. For instance, you can check multiple conditions using combinations of AND, OR, and NOT:```javascript: let temperature = 72; let isSunny = true; if (temperature > 70 && isSunny || !is Raining) { console. log('It is a nice day.');}```

In this example, the message will be logged if the temperature is greater than 70 and it is sunny or not raining.

Logical operators are fundamental for writing sophisticated control structures in your programs. They enable you to create complex conditions that guide the execution flow, making your applications more dynamic and responsive to various scenarios.

In summary, operators and expressions are essential components of JavaScript that allow you to perform computations, compare values, and control the flow of your programs. Arithmetic operators enable you to handle numerical data through basic mathematical operations. Comparison operators allow you to compare values and make decisions based on those comparisons. Logical operators let you combine multiple conditions to create complex logic for controlling program flow. Mastering these operators and understanding how to use them in expressions is crucial for writing efficient, effective, and maintainable JavaScript code. As you gain proficiency with these fundamental tools, you will be better equipped to tackle more advanced programming challenges and build dynamic, interactive web applications.

Working with Strings and Numbers

In the realm of programming, strings, and numbers represent two of the most fundamental data types. Each serves distinct purposes and offers a variety of methods and operations to facilitate complex tasks. Understanding how to manipulate strings and perform number operations is crucial for any programmer, as these skills are integral to developing efficient and effective code.

Strings, sequences of characters, are used to represent text in programming. They are immutable in many programming languages, meaning once a string is created, it cannot be altered. However, numerous methods and functions are available to manipulate and work with strings, enabling programmers to perform various operations.

String concatenation is one of the most basic operations. It involves joining two or more strings end-to-end to form a new string. This can be achieved in many languages using the `+` operator or specific concatenation functions. For instance, in Python, you can concatenate strings using the `+` operator (`"Hello" + " " + "World"` results in `"Hello World"`).

Another joint manipulation is slicing, which allows extracting a part of a string. Slicing involves specifying a start and end index and returning the substring within that range. For example, the expression `"Hello World" [0:5]` in Python would return `"Hello".` This operation is essential for tasks such as parsing text files or processing user input.

String formatting is also a crucial technique, enabling the insertion of variables into strings. This can be done using methods such as concatenation, the `format()` method, or f-strings (formatted string literals) in Python. For example, an f-string allows embedding expressions inside string literals using curly braces (`f"Hello, {name}"`).

Strings also offer a variety of methods for modifying their content or querying information. The `upper()` and `lower()` methods return new strings with all characters converted to uppercase or lowercase. The `replace()` method allows replacing all occurrences of a substring with another substring (`"Hello World". Replace("World," "Python")` results in `"Hello Python"`). The `split()` method divides a string into a list of substrings based on a specified delimiter. At the same time, the `join()` method performs the reverse operation, combining a list of strings into a single string with a specified separator.

Searching within strings is another essential task. Methods like `find()` and `index()` return the position of the first occurrence of a substring, while `count()` returns the number of occurrences. Regular expressions, supported in many languages through libraries or built-in modules, provide powerful pattern-matching capabilities, enabling complex searches and text manipulations.

Numbers, encompassing integers, floating-point numbers, and sometimes more complex types like decimals and fractions, are pivotal in programming for performing calculations and representing numerical data. Fundamental arithmetic operations include addition, subtraction, multiplication, and division. These are typically performed using operators such as `+,` `-,` `*,` and `/.`

Beyond basic arithmetic, programming languages provide many functions and methods for more advanced mathematical operations. The `math` module in Python, for instance, includes functions for trigonometric operations (`sin(),` `cos(),` `tan()`), logarithmic functions (`log(),` `log10()`), and constants like π (`pi`). These functions are essential for applications ranging from scientific computing to game development.

Rounding numbers is an everyday necessity. The `round()` function rounds a number to a specified number of decimal places. Additionally, the `floor()` and `ceil()` functions from the `math` module round numbers down or up to the nearest integer, respectively. These methods are crucial when dealing with currency calculations, measurements, or any scenario requiring precise control over numerical accuracy.

Random number generation is another critical aspect, particularly in simulations, games, and security. The `random` module in Python provides functions to generate pseudo-random numbers. The `radiant ()` function returns a random integer within a specified range, while `random()` generates a random float between 0 and 1. For more complex randomizations, functions like `choice()` can select random elements from a list, and `shuffle()` can randomly reorder the elements of a list.

Type conversion between strings and numbers is often necessary in programming. For example, user input is typically received as a string and must be converted to a numerical type for arithmetic operations. Functions like `int()` and `float()` in Python convert strings to integers and floating-point numbers, respectively. Conversely, `str()` converts numbers to their string representation, facilitating tasks such as generating reports or displaying results to users.

Handling numbers also involves understanding numerical precision and representation. Floating-point numbers are represented in a way that can introduce rounding errors due to their binary nature. This limitation necessitates careful handling, especially in financial and scientific applications. Python's `decimal` module provides the `Decimal` type for decimal floating-point arithmetic, offering higher precision and control over rounding behavior than the standard float type.

In conclusion, mastering string manipulation and number operations is foundational for effective programming. With their vast array of methods, Strings allow for versatile text processing and manipulation, while numbers and their associated operations enable a wide range of calculations and numerical analyses. Together, these skills empower programmers to tackle diverse challenges, from simple data entry tasks to complex scientific computations. Understanding and leveraging the capabilities of strings and numbers is essential for developing robust and efficient software solutions.

CHAPTER III

Control Structures

Conditional Statements

Looping constructs are essential components in programming that allow for the repeated execution of a block of code. These constructs are particularly useful for tasks that require iteration, such as processing items in a list, performing operations a certain number of times, or handling repetitive input. The primary looping constructs include `for` loops, `while` loops, and `do...while` loops. Each of these constructs serves a specific purpose and has distinct characteristics that make them suitable for different scenarios.

A `for` loop is one of the most commonly used looping constructs. It is ideal for scenarios where the number of iterations is known beforehand. The syntax of a `for` loop typically includes three parts: initialization, condition, and increment/decrement. The loop begins with initializing a loop control variable, often used to track the number of iterations. The condition is evaluated before each iteration, and the loop body executes if the condition is proper. After the loop body executes, the control variable is updated (incremented or decremented), and the condition is re-evaluated. This process repeats until the condition evaluates to false.

For example, a `for` loop might look like this in Python: Python: for i in range(10): print(i).

In this example, the loop initializes `i` to 0 and increments it by one after each iteration, printing the value of `i` until `i` reaches 9. The `range(10)` function generates numbers from 0 to 9; the loop iterates over this sequence.

`For` loops help iterate over collections such as lists, arrays, or other iterable objects. For instance, iterating through a list of items can be easily accomplished using a `for` loop: Python: fruits = ["apple," "banana," "cherry"]: for fruit in fruits: print(fruit)

In this case, the loop iterates over each element in the `fruits` list, printing each fruit.

While `for` loops are excellent for scenarios where the number of iterations is predetermined, `while` loops are better suited for situations where the number of iterations is not known in advance. A `while` loop repeatedly executes a code block once a specified condition evaluates to true. The condition is checked before each iteration, and the loop terminates if it evaluates to false.

The syntax of a `while` loop in Python is straightforward: python: i = 0: while i < 10: print(i): i += 1

In this example, the loop initializes `i' to 0 and continues to execute as long as `i' is less than 10. After each iteration, `i' is incremented by 1. This loop functions similarly to the previous `for` loop example, but the iteration control is explicitly managed within the loop body.

`While` loops are helpful when the loop's continuation depends on a condition that might change within the loop body, such as user input or the result of a computation. For instance, a `while` loop can be used to read user input until a specific condition is met: Python: user_input = while user_input != "exit": user_input = input("Enter a command (type 'exit' to quit): "): print(f "You entered: {user_input}")

In this scenario, the loop prompts the user for input until the user types "exit."

The `do...while` loop, although not present in Python but available in languages like C, C++, and Java, is similar to the `while` loop but with one key difference: the loop body executes at least once before the condition is evaluated. This guarantees that the code inside the loop runs at least once, regardless of whether the condition is initially true or false.

The syntax of a `do...while` loop in C++ looks like this: cpp: int i = 0; do {cout << i << endl; i++;} while (i < 10);

In this example, the loop initializes `i' to 0, prints the value of `i', increments ` i', and then checks the condition. The loop will continue to execute as long as `i' is less than 10. Even if `i' were initially greater than or equal to 10, the loop body would execute once before the condition is evaluated.

The `do...while` loop is handy when the code inside the loop must execute at least once, such as in menu-driven programs where the user needs to see the menu at least once before selecting.

In summary, looping constructs such as `for` loops, `while` loops, and `do...while` loops are fundamental tools in programming for performing repetitive tasks. `For` loops are ideal when the number of iterations is known beforehand and are commonly used for iterating over collections. `While` loops are better suited for situations where the continuation of the loop depends on a condition that may change within the loop body. Although not available in Python, the `do...while` loop guarantees that the loop body executes at least once, making it useful for scenarios where initial execution is necessary regardless of the condition.

Understanding the appropriate use cases for each loop type is crucial for writing efficient and effective code. Proper use of looping constructs can lead to more readable and maintainable programs and enable complex tasks to be performed with relative ease. Mastering these constructs is essential for any programmer, allowing them to implement logic that requires iteration and repeated execution efficiently.

Looping Constructs

Defining and calling functions are fundamental aspects of programming that enable the creation of reusable and modular code. Functions allow programmers to encapsulate a sequence of instructions into a single logical unit, which can be executed as often as needed without rewriting the code. Understanding how to declare functions and the differences between function declarations and function expressions is crucial for effective coding.

```python
def calculate_factorial(n):
    result = 1
    if n == 0 or n == 1:
        return result
    while n > 1:
        result = result * n
        n = n - 1
    return result

calculate_factorial(1)
1
calculate_factorial(5)
120
calculate_factorial(10)
3628800
```

Function declarations, or function definitions, are the most straightforward way to create a function. In most programming languages, a function declaration specifies the function's name, parameters, and the block of code that constitutes the function's body. The syntax varies slightly between languages, but the core concept remains the same. For example, in Python, a function is declared using the `def` keyword followed by the function's name and a set of parentheses containing any parameters. The function's code block is indented below the declaration. Here is a simple example: Python: def greet(name): print(f"Hello, {name}!")

In this example, the `greet` function takes one parameter, `name,` and prints a greeting message. To call this function, you use its name followed by parentheses, passing any required arguments: Python: greet("Alice"). This call would output: `Hello, Alice!`

Function declarations are hoisted to the top of their scope in languages like JavaScript, meaning they can be called before they are defined in the code. For example: javascript: console.log(square(5)); function square(number) {return number * number;}

In this JavaScript example, the `square` function is called before its declaration, but due to hoisting, this code works correctly and outputs `25`.

Function expressions, on the other hand, involve creating a function and assigning it to a variable. This method provides more flexibility in terms of function usage and scope. A function expression can be named or anonymous. Named function expressions are helpful for recursion or debugging, while anonymous function expressions are commonly used in situations like passing a function as an argument to another function.

Here is an example of an anonymous function expression in JavaScript: javascript: const greet = function(name: {console. log(`Hello, ${name}!`);};greet("Bob");

This example assigns an anonymous function to the variable `greet` and then calls it. Function expressions are not hoisted, so they cannot be called before they are defined in the code.

In addition to anonymous function expressions, modern JavaScript supports arrow functions, a more concise syntax for writing function expressions. Arrow functions are handy for short functions and callbacks. Here is an example: javascript: const square = (number) => number * number; console.log(square(4)).

In this example, the arrow function syntax `(number) => number * number` defines a function that takes one parameter and returns its square. Arrow functions have a more concise syntax and do not bind their own `this` value, making them suitable for many functional programming patterns.

Functions can also be declared within other functions, creating what are known as nested functions or inner functions. These functions have access to the variables and parameters of their containing (outer) function. This feature is useful for creating helper functions that are only relevant within the context of the outer function. For example, in Python: Python: def outer function(text): def inner_function(): print(text): inner function() outer function("Hello from the outer function")

In this example, `inner function` is defined within `outer_function` and can access the `text` variable from its containing scope. When `outer_function` is called, it calls `inner_function,` which prints the text.

Functions can also return other functions, enabling the creation of higher-order functions. Higher-order functions either take other functions as arguments or return them as results. This is a powerful feature that allows for greater abstraction and code reuse. For example, in JavaScript: javascript: function create greeting(greeting) {return function(name) {console.log(`${greeting}, ${name}!`);};}

Const greetHello = create greeting("Hello"); greetHello("Charlie");

Here, `create greeting` returns a new function incorporating the specified greeting. The `greetHello` variable holds this returned function, which can be called with a name to produce a personalized greeting.

Another important concept in defining and calling functions is using default parameters. Default parameters allow functions to have parameters that assume a default value if no argument is provided. This can simplify function calls and provide more flexible APIs. For example, in Python: Python

```
def greet(name, greeting="Hello"):print(f"{greeting}, {name}!") greet("Dave"): greet("Eve," "Hi")
```

In this example, the `greeting` parameter has a default value of `"Hello,"` so when `greet` is called with only one argument, it uses the default greeting. When both arguments are provided, the specified greeting is used instead.

In JavaScript, default parameters work similarly: javascript: function greet(name, greeting = "Hello") {console.log({greeting},{name}!`);}greet("Frank");greet("Grace", "Hi").

Both function declarations and function expressions can utilize default parameters, enhancing flexibility and usability.

Furthermore, functions in many languages support variadic parameters, which allow them to accept an arbitrary number of arguments. This is useful when the number of inputs can vary. For example, in Python, the `*args` syntax is used:

Python: def add(*numbers): return sum(numbers): print(add(1, 2, 3, 4))

In this example, the `add` function can take any number of numerical arguments and return their sum. Similarly, in JavaScript, the rest parameter syntax (`...args`) is used: javascript: function add(...numbers) { return numbers.reduce((sum, num) => sum + num, 0);}console.log(add(1, 2, 3, 4));

Both examples demonstrate how variadic parameters can make functions more adaptable to different input scenarios.

In conclusion, understanding how to define and call functions is essential for any programmer. Function declarations provide a straightforward way to create reusable code blocks, while function expressions offer greater flexibility and control over the scope and timing of function definitions. Both approaches have advantages and appropriate use cases, and modern programming languages often provide additional features like arrow functions, default parameters, and variadic parameters to enhance the power and usability of functions. Mastery of these concepts allows for creating efficient, readable, and maintainable code, forming the foundation of practical software development.

Controlling Loop Execution

In programming, understanding how to pass arguments to functions and return values from them is crucial for writing effective and modular code. Parameters and return values allow functions to interact with the rest of the program, making them versatile and reusable. This process involves defining the inputs (parameters) a function can accept and specifying the outputs (return values) it produces.

Passing arguments to functions begins with defining the parameters in the function declaration. Parameters are placeholders for the actual values (arguments) passed when the function is called. These parameters are used within the function to perform operations or calculations. For example, in Python, a simple function that adds two numbers can be defined as follows: Python: def add(a, b): return a + b.

In this example, `a' and `b` are parameters. When the function `add` is called with two arguments, `add(3, 5)`, the values `3` and `5` are passed to the parameters ` a' and `b,` respectively. The function then returns their sum, `8`.

Arguments can be passed to functions in various ways, including positional, keyword, and default arguments. Positional arguments are the most straightforward method, where the order of the arguments in the function call matches the order of the parameters in the function definition. For instance: Python result = add(10, 20).

Here, `10` is passed to `a' and `20` to `b,` resulting in the function returning `30`.

Keyword arguments, however, allow for greater flexibility by specifying the parameter names and their corresponding values. This method is beneficial when a function has many parameters, or you want to clarify which values are assigned to which parameters. For example: python: result = add(a=10, b=20)

This call produces the same result as the previous example but is more explicit about which values are assigned to which parameters.

Default arguments enable a function to have parameters with default values, which are used if no corresponding argument is provided in the function call. This makes functions more versatile and can simplify function calls. For instance: python: def greet(name, greeting="Hello"):

return   f"{greeting},   {name}!"   print(greet("Alice")):
print(greet("Bob," "Hi")).

In this example, the `greet` function has a default value of `"Hello"` for the `greeting` parameter. When called with only one argument, the function uses the default greeting. If a second argument is provided, it overrides the default value.

Variadic parameters allow a function to accept an arbitrary number of arguments and provide additional flexibility. In Python, the `args` syntax collects multiple positional arguments into a tuple, while `kwargs` collects multiple keyword arguments into a dictionary. For example: python

def sum_all(args): return sum(args): print(sum_all(1, 2, 3, 4, 5))

In this example, `sum_all` can accept any number of arguments and returns their sum. Similarly, `kwargs` allows handling an arbitrary number of keyword arguments: Python: def print_info(kwargs): for key, value in kwargs.items(): print(f"{key}: {value}") print_info(name="Alice", age=30, city="New York").

Here, `print_info` prints out all the provided keyword arguments, regardless of how many are passed.

Returning values from functions is equally essential as passing arguments. The `return` statement returns a value to the caller, allowing functions to produce output that can be used elsewhere in the program. A function can return any data type, including numbers, strings, lists, dictionaries, and other functions.

For example, a function that returns the square of a number in Python might look like this: Python: def square(x): return x * x.

Calling `square(4)` would return `16`. A function can also return multiple values using tuples, a powerful feature for packing and unpacking data. For instance: python: def get_min_max(numbers): return min(numbers), max(numbers): min_val, max_val = get_min_max([1, 2, 3, 4, 5]): print(min_val, max_val).

In this example, `get_min_max` returns a list's minimum and maximum values, which can then be unpacked into separate variables.

Functions can also return other functions, enabling higher-order functions and more advanced programming techniques. This is particularly useful in functional programming paradigms. For example: python: def create_multiplier(factor): def multiplier(x): return x factor: return multiplier: times_two = create_multiplier(2): print(times_two(5)).

Here, `create_multiplier` returns a new function `multiplier` that multiplies its input by the specified `factor.` The returned function can then be used independently.

In addition to returning simple values or other functions, functions can return complex data structures like lists and dictionaries. This capability allows for the encapsulation and manipulation of data within functions before returning the processed results. For example: python: def process_data(data): processed = [x * 2 for x in data if x > 0]: return processed: result = process_data([1, -2, 3, 0, 4]): print(result).

In this example, `process_data` processes a list of numbers, doubling the positive values and returning the resulting list.

In some languages, functions can have a void return type, meaning they do not return any value. These functions typically perform actions such as printing output or modifying the global state. For instance, in C++: cpp: void print_hello() {std::cout << "Hello, World!" << std::endl;}: print_hello().

Here, `print_hello` does not return a value but acts (printing to the console).

Understanding the mechanisms of passing arguments to functions and returning values from them is fundamental to writing modular, reusable, and maintainable code. Parameters allow functions to accept varying inputs, making them flexible and adaptable to different contexts. Return values enable functions to produce output that can be used elsewhere in the program, facilitating data flow and control.

In summary, parameters and return values are critical components of function definitions that enhance the functionality and versatility of functions. By passing arguments, functions can operate on different data inputs, while return values allow functions to produce valuable outputs. Various techniques, such as positional arguments, keyword arguments, default arguments, and variadic parameters, provide flexibility in how functions are called and how they interact with the rest of the program. Similarly, the ability to return multiple values, complex data structures, and even other functions allows for powerful and sophisticated programming paradigms. Mastery of these concepts is essential for effective software development, enabling the creation of robust, efficient, and reusable code.

CHAPTER IV

Functions

Defining and Calling Functions

Defining and calling functions are fundamental aspects of programming that enable the creation of reusable and modular code. Functions allow programmers to encapsulate a sequence of instructions into a single logical unit, which can be executed as often as needed without rewriting the code. Understanding how to declare functions and the differences between function declarations and function expressions is crucial for effective coding.

Function declarations, or function definitions, are the most straightforward way to create a function. In most programming languages, a function declaration specifies the function's name, parameters, and the block of code that constitutes the function's body. The syntax varies slightly between languages, but the core concept remains the same. For example, in Python, a function is declared using the `def` keyword followed by the function's name and a set of parentheses containing any parameters. The function's code block is indented below the declaration. Here is a simple example: Python: def greet(name): print(f"Hello, {name}!")

In this example, the `greet` function takes one parameter, `name,` and prints a greeting message. To call this function, you simply use its name followed by parentheses, passing any required arguments: Python: greet("Alice")

This call would output: `Hello, Alice!`

Function declarations are hoisted to the top of their scope in languages like JavaScript, meaning they can be called before they are defined in the code. For example: javascript

console.log(square(5)); function square(number) { return number * number;}

In this JavaScript example, the `square` function is called before its declaration, but due to hoisting, this code works correctly and outputs `25`.

Function expressions, on the other hand, involve creating a function and assigning it to a variable. This method provides more flexibility in terms of function usage and scope. A function expression can be named or anonymous. Named function expressions are helpful for recursion or debugging, while anonymous function expressions are commonly used in situations like passing a function as an argument to another function.

Here is an example of an anonymous function expression in JavaScript: javascript: const greet = function(name) { console. log(`Hello, ${name}!`);}; greet("Bob");

This example assigns an anonymous function to the variable `greet` and then calls it. Function expressions are not hoisted, so they cannot be called before they are defined in the code.

In addition to anonymous function expressions, modern JavaScript supports arrow functions, a more concise syntax for writing function expressions. Arrow functions are handy for short functions and callbacks. Here is an example: javascript: const square = (number) => number * number; console.log(square(4)):

In this example, the arrow function syntax `(number) => number * number` defines a function that takes one parameter and returns its square. Arrow functions have a more concise syntax and do not bind their own `this` value, making them suitable for many functional programming patterns.

Functions can also be declared within other functions, creating what are known as nested functions or inner functions. These functions have access to the variables and parameters of their containing (outer) function. This feature helps create helper functions that are only relevant within the context of the outer function. For example, in Python:

Python: def outer_function(text): def inner_function(): print(text): inner_function(): outer_function("Hello from the outer function")

In this example, `inner_function` is defined within `outer_function` and can access the `text` variable from its containing scope. When `outer_function` is called, it calls `inner_function,` which prints the text.

Functions can also return other functions, enabling the creation of higher-order functions. Higher-order functions either take other functions as arguments or return them as results. This is a powerful feature that allows for greater abstraction and code reuse. For example, in JavaScript: javascript: function create greeting(greeting) {return function(name) {console.log(`${greeting}, ${name}!`);};}

Const greetHello = create greeting("Hello");

Great hello("Charlie").

Here, `create greeting` returns a new function incorporating the specified greeting. The `greetHello` variable holds this returned function, which can be called with a name to produce a personalized greeting.

Another important concept in defining and calling functions is using default parameters. Default parameters allow functions to have parameters that assume a default value if no argument is provided. This can simplify function calls and provide more flexible APIs. For example, in Python:

Python: def greet(name, greeting="Hello"): print(f"{greeting}, {name}!") greet("Dave") greet("Eve," "Hi")

In this example, the `greeting` parameter has a default value of `"Hello,"` so when `greet` is called with only one argument, it uses the default greeting. When both arguments are provided, the specified greeting is used instead.

In JavaScript, default parameters work similarly: javascript: function greet(name, greeting = "Hello") {console. log(`${greeting}, ${name}!`);}

Greet("Frank");greet("Grace", "Hi").

Both function declarations and function expressions can utilize default parameters, enhancing flexibility and usability.

Furthermore, functions in many languages support variadic parameters, which allow them to accept an arbitrary number of arguments. This is useful when the number of inputs can vary. For example, in Python, the `args` syntax is used: Python: def add(numbers): return sum(numbers): print(add(1, 2, 3, 4)).

In this example, the `add` function can take any number of numerical arguments and return their sum. Similarly, in JavaScript, the rest parameter syntax (`...args`) is used:

javascript: function add(...numbers) { return numbers.reduce((sum, num) => sum + num, 0);} Console.log(add(1, 2, 3, 4)).

Both examples demonstrate how variadic parameters can make functions more adaptable to different input scenarios.

In conclusion, understanding how to define and call functions is essential for any programmer. Function declarations provide a straightforward way to create reusable code blocks, while function expressions offer greater flexibility and control over the scope and timing of function definitions. Both approaches have advantages and appropriate use cases, and modern programming languages often provide additional features like arrow functions, default parameters, and variadic parameters to enhance the power and usability of functions. Mastery of these concepts allows for creating efficient, readable, and maintainable code, forming the foundation of practical software development.

Parameters and Return Values

In programming, understanding how to pass arguments to functions and return values from them is crucial for writing effective and modular code. Parameters and return values allow functions to interact with the rest of the program, making them versatile and reusable. This process involves defining the inputs (parameters) a function can accept and specifying the outputs (return values) it produces.

Passing arguments to functions begins with defining the parameters in the function declaration. Parameters are placeholders for the actual values (arguments) passed when the function is called. These parameters are used within the function to perform operations or calculations. For example, in Python, a simple function that adds two numbers can be defined as follows: Python: def add(a, b): return a + b.

In this example, `a' and `b` are parameters. When the function `add` is called with two arguments, `add(3, 5)`, the values `3` and `5` are passed to the parameters ` a' and `b`, respectively. The function then returns their sum, `8`.

Arguments can be passed to functions in various ways, including positional, keyword, and default arguments. Positional arguments are the most straightforward method, where the order of the arguments in the function call matches the order of the parameters in the function definition. For instance: Python: result = add(10, 20).

Here, `10` is passed to `a' and `20` to `b,` resulting in the function returning `30`.

Keyword arguments, however, allow for greater flexibility by specifying the parameter names and their corresponding values. This method is beneficial when a function has many parameters, or you want to clarify which values are assigned to which parameters. For example: Python: result = add(a=10, b=20).

This call produces the same result as the previous example but is more explicit about which values are assigned to which parameters.

Default arguments enable a function to have parameters with default values, which are used if no corresponding argument is provided in the function call. This makes functions more versatile and can simplify function calls. For instance: Python: def greet(name, greeting="Hello"): return f"{greeting}, {name}!" print(greet("Alice")): print(greet("Bob," "Hi")).

In this example, the `greet` function has a default value of `"Hello"` for the `greeting` parameter. When called with only one argument, the function uses the default greeting. If a second argument is provided, it overrides the default value.

Variadic parameters allow a function to accept an arbitrary number of arguments and provide additional flexibility. In Python, the `args` syntax collects multiple positional arguments into a tuple, while `kwargs` collects multiple keyword arguments into a dictionary. For example, Python: def sum_all(args): return sum(args): print(sum_all(1, 2, 3, 4, 5).

In this example, `sum_all` can accept any number of arguments and returns their sum. Similarly, `kwargs` allows handling an arbitrary number of keyword arguments: Python: def print_info(kwargs): for key, value in kwargs.items(): print(f"{key}: {value}"): print_info(name="Alice", age=30, city="New York")

Here, `print_info` prints out all the provided keyword arguments, regardless of how many are passed.

Returning values from functions is equally essential as passing arguments. The `return` statement returns a value to the caller, allowing functions to produce output that can be used elsewhere in the program. A function can return any data type, including numbers, strings, lists, dictionaries, and other functions.

For example, a function that returns the square of a number in Python might look like this: Python: def square(x): return x * x.

Calling `square(4)` would return `16`. A function can also return multiple values using tuples, a powerful feature for packing and unpacking data. For instance: Python: def get_min_max(numbers): return min(numbers), max(numbers): min_val, max_val = get_min_max([1, 2, 3, 4, 5]): print(min_val, max_val).

In this example, `get_min_max` returns a list's minimum and maximum values, which can then be unpacked into separate variables.

Functions can also return other functions, enabling higher-order functions and more advanced programming techniques. This is particularly useful in functional programming paradigms. For example: Python: def create_multiplier(factor): def multiplier(x): return x factor: return multiplier: times_two = create_multiplier(2): print(times_two(5)).

Here, `create_multiplier` returns a new function `multiplier` that multiplies its input by the specified `factor.` The returned function can then be used independently.

In addition to returning simple values or other functions, functions can return complex data structures like lists and dictionaries. This capability allows for the encapsulation and manipulation of data within functions before returning the processed results. For example: Python: def process_data(data): processed = [x * 2 for x in data if x > 0]return processed: result = process_data([1, -2, 3, 0, 4])print(result)

In this example, `process_data` processes a list of numbers, doubling the positive values and returning the resulting list.

In some languages, functions can have a void return type, meaning they do not return any value. These functions typically perform actions such as printing output or modifying the global state. For instance, in C++: cpp void print_hello() {std::cout << "Hello, World!" << std::endl;}print_hello().

Here, `print_hello` does not return a value but acts (printing to the console).

Understanding the mechanisms of passing arguments to functions and returning values from them is fundamental to writing modular, reusable, and maintainable code. Parameters allow functions to accept varying inputs, making them flexible and adaptable to different contexts. Return values enable functions to produce output that can be used elsewhere in the program, facilitating data flow and control.

In summary, parameters and return values are critical components of function definitions that enhance the functionality and versatility of functions. By passing arguments, functions can operate on different data inputs, while return values allow functions to produce valuable outputs. Various techniques, such as positional arguments, keyword arguments, default arguments, and variadic parameters, provide flexibility in how functions are called and how they interact with the rest of the program. Similarly, the ability to return multiple values, complex data structures, and even other functions allows for powerful and sophisticated programming paradigms. Mastery of these concepts is essential for effective software development, enabling the creation of robust, efficient, and reusable code.

Scope and Closures

Understanding scope and closures is essential for mastering programming languages, especially those that support functional and object-oriented paradigms like JavaScript and Python. Scope refers to the context within which variables and functions can be accessed or referenced. It determines the visibility and lifecycle of variables. Closures, on the other hand, are a feature that allows a function to remember the environment in which it was created, even after that environment has disappeared. This powerful concept is central to many advanced programming techniques.

Global and local scopes are the two primary types of scope in most programming languages. Global scope refers to the outermost scope of a program, where variables and functions declared here are accessible from anywhere within the program. Conversely, local scope pertains to variables declared within a function, accessible only within that function. This distinction helps manage variable lifetimes and avoid naming conflicts.

In Python, for example, a variable declared outside any function is in the global scope: Python x = 10 # global scope. def foo(): print(x) # accesses global x. foo() # prints 10: print(x) # prints 10

Here, `x` is a global variable accessible inside and outside the function ` foo'.

However, when a variable is declared within a function, it resides in the local scope: Python: def foo(): y = 5 # local scope: print(y).

foo() # prints 5: print(y) # raises Name Error: name 'y' is not defined

In this case, `y' is local to `foo' and cannot be accessed outside.

JavaScript demonstrates similar principles of scope: javascript: let x = 10; // global scope. function foo() { console.log(x); // accesses global x}

foo(); // prints 10 console.log(x); // prints 10

Here, `x` is globally scoped and thus accessible inside the function ` foo'. Declaring a variable within a function creates a local scope: javascript: function foo() { let y = 5; // local scope console.log(y);}.

foo(); // prints 5: console.log(y); // raises Reference Error: y is not defined

The variable ` y' is local to the function ` foo' and cannot be accessed outside of it.

A crucial scope aspect is understanding how functions handle variable access and closures. A closure is created when a function captures variables from its surrounding scope. This allows the function to access these variables after executing the outer function. Closures enable powerful programming patterns, such as function factories and private variables.

Consider the following example in JavaScript: javascript

function make counter() {let count = 0; // local variable return function() {count += 1; return count;};} const counter = make counter();

console.log(counter()); // prints 1

console.log(counter()); // prints 2

console.log(counter()); // prints 3

In this example, `make_counter` creates a local variable `count` and returns an anonymous function. This returned function forms a closure, capturing `count` and retaining access even after `make Counter` has completed execution. Each call to `counter` increments and returns the updated value of `count.`

Python also supports closures: Python: def make_counter(): count = 0 # local variable: def counter(): nonlocal count: count += 1 return count: return counter:

counter = make_counter()

print(counter()) # prints 1

print(counter()) # prints 2

print(counter()) # prints 3

Here, `make counter` defines a local variable `count` and returns the nested `counter` function. The `nonlocal` keyword allows `counter` to modify the `count` variable in the enclosing scope. Each call to `counter` updates and returns the value of `count.`

Closures are handy for data encapsulation and creating function factories. They enable the creation of private variables and methods, which can only be accessed through specific functions. This technique is fundamental in object-oriented programming for creating private properties and methods.

Another powerful use of closures is in callback functions, especially in asynchronous programming. In JavaScript, closures are frequently used to maintain state within callbacks: javascript: function create Greeter(greeting) {return function(name) {console. log(`${greeting}, ${name}!`);};}

const greetHello = create Greeter("Hello");

greetHello("Alice"); // prints "Hello, Alice!"

greetHello("Bob"); // prints "Hello, Bob!"

In this example, `create Greeter` returns a function that captures the `greeting` variable, allowing the returned function to access `greeting` each time it is called, even though `create Greeter` has already finished executing.

In Python, closures are similarly helpful for creating function factories and maintaining state: Python: def create_greeter(greeting): def greet(name): print(f" {greeting}, {name}!"): return greet

greet_hello = create_greeter("Hello")

greet_hello("Alice") # prints "Hello, Alice!"

greet_hello("Bob") # prints "Hello, Bob!"

The `create_greeter` function returns a nested `greet` function that captures the `greeting` variable, enabling persistent access to `greeting.`

Understanding closures also involves grasping the concept of lexical scoping, where the scope of a variable is determined by its position within the source code. Python and JavaScript use lexical scoping, meaning variables' visibility is defined at compile time based on their location in the source code.

Consider the following JavaScript example to illustrate lexical scoping:

javascript: let x = 10; function outer() { let x = 20; function inner() {console.log(x); // accesses x from outer scope }inner();}outer(); // prints 20.

In this example, the `inner` function accesses `x` from its nearest enclosing scope, the `outer` function's scope. Lexical scoping ensures that the value of `x` in `inner` is determined by its location in the code, not by the call stack or the execution context.

```
function outerFunc() {
    let outerVar = 'I am outside!';
                ↑ Captured

    function innerFunc() {                    Closure
        outerVar; // => "I am outside!"
    }

    return innerFunc;
}

function exec() {
    const myInnerFunc = outerFunc();
    myInnerFunc();
}

exec();
```

Similarly, in Python: Python: x = 10: def outer(): x = 20: def inner(): print(x) # accesses x from outer scope: inner() outer() # prints 20

The `inner` function accesses the `x` variable from its nearest enclosing scope, which is the `outer` function's scope, demonstrating lexical scoping.

Closures and lexical scoping enable powerful programming patterns, but they also require careful management of variable lifetimes and references to avoid common pitfalls like memory leaks in long-running applications. Understanding the underlying principles of scope and closures equips developers with the tools to write more efficient, maintainable, and modular code.

In conclusion, scope and closures are fundamental to programming, particularly in languages that support functional and object-oriented paradigms. Global and local scopes define the accessibility of variables and functions within a program, helping to manage variable lifetimes and avoid naming conflicts. Closures extend the utility of tasks by allowing them to capture and remember variables from their containing scope, even after that scope has existed. This capability is essential for creating function factories, maintaining state in callbacks, and encapsulating data. By mastering scope and closures, programmers can write more flexible, efficient, and maintainable code, leveraging these powerful concepts to build complex and sophisticated applications.

CHAPTER V

Objects and Arrays

Introduction to Objects

Objects are a fundamental concept in many programming languages, particularly those that support object-oriented programming (OOP) paradigms, such as JavaScript, Python, Java, and C++. An object collects related data and functions organized as properties and methods. This encapsulation allows for a modular approach to programming, where data and behavior are bundled together, facilitating code reuse, readability, and maintenance. Understanding how to create, manipulate, and utilize objects is crucial for effective programming.

Creating objects varies slightly between languages but follows a common conceptual framework. Objects can be created in JavaScript using object literals, constructors, or the `class` syntax introduced in ECMAScript 6. An object literal is a simple and direct way to create objects. For example:

Javascript: let Person = {name: "Alice" age: 30, greet: function() {console.log("Hello, my name is " + this. name);}};

In this example, `person` is an object with properties `name` and `age` and a method `greet.` The method is a function associated with the `person` object and can access the object's properties using the `this` keyword. To call the `greet` method, you would use `Person. Greet ()` outputs "Hello, my name is Alice."

JavaScript also allows the creation of objects using constructors, functions designed to initialize new objects. Here's an example:

javascript: function Person(name, age) { this.name = name; this. Age = age; this. Greet = function() {console.log("Hello, my name is " + this.name);};}

let person1 = new Person("Bob", 25);person1.greet(); // Outputs: "Hello, my name is Bob."

In this example, `Person` is a constructor function that initializes properties `name` and `age` and defines the `greet` method. The `new` keyword creates a new instance of `Person`.

With the introduction of classes in ECMAScript 6, JavaScript provides a more structured syntax for defining objects: javascript

class Person { constructor(name, age) { this.name = name;this.age = age;}greet() {console.log("Hello, my name is " + this.name);}}let person2 = new Person("Charlie", 28);person2.greet(); // Outputs: "Hello, my name is Charlie." Here, the `Person` class encapsulates the properties and methods, providing a blueprint for creating objects.

In Python, objects are similarly created using classes. A class in Python defines the blueprint for objects, encapsulating properties and methods. Here's an example: Python: Class Person: def __init__(self, name, age): self. Name = name: self. Age = age: def greet(self):print(f"Hello, my name is {self.name}"): person1 = Person("Alice", 30): person1.greet() # Outputs: "Hello, my name is Alice."

In this example, the `Person` class defines the `__init__` method, initializing the object's properties, and a `greet` method. Creating an instance of `Person` and calling `greet` functions similarly to JavaScript.

Manipulating objects involves accessing and modifying their properties and invoking their methods. In

JavaScript, you can access properties using dot or bracket notation: javascript: Console.log(Person. name); // Outputs: "Alice." Person.age = 31.: Console.log(person["age"]); // Outputs: 31

Dot notation is the most common way to access properties, but bracket notation is functional when property names are dynamic or not valid identifiers.

Python provides similar mechanisms for property access and modification: python: print(person1.name) # Outputs: "Alice": Person1.age = 31: print(person1.age) # Outputs: 31

Object methods are functions that operate on the object's properties. In JavaScript, methods can be added to objects anytime: javascript: Person. Say goodbye = function() {console.log("Goodbye from " + this.name);};person. Say goodbye(); // Outputs: "Goodbye from Alice."

This flexibility allows for dynamic enhancement of objects, although it's typically better practice to define all methods within the object's constructor or class definition.

In Python, methods are defined within the class, but you can also add methods dynamically: Python: def say goodbye(self): print(goodbye from {self. name}"): Person. Say goodbye = say goodbye

Person1.say_goodbye() # Outputs: "Goodbye from Alice"

Properties in objects can be more than simple data attributes. They can also be computed dynamically using getter and setter methods. JavaScript supports this with the `get` and `set` keywords: javascript: class Rectangle {constructor(width, height) {this.width = width;this.height = height;}get area() {return this.width * this.height;}set area(value) {console.log("Area is a derived property; cannot set directly.");}}let rect = new

Rectangle(10, 20);console.log(rect.area); // Outputs: 200

Rect.area = 300; // Outputs: "Area is a derived property; cannot set directly."

Here, the `area` property is computed based on the object's dimensions, demonstrating how derived properties can encapsulate more complex logic.

Python achieves similar functionality with property decorators: Python

Class Rectangle: def __init__(self, width, height):self. Width = width self.height = height property: def area(self): return self. Width * self.height: rect = Rectangle(10, 20) print(rect.area) # Outputs: 200

The `@property` decorator allows the `area` method to be accessed as an attribute, providing a clean interface for computed properties.

Encapsulation, one of the core principles of OOP, is exemplified by objects and their methods and properties. It allows for bundling data (properties) and behavior (methods) while restricting direct access to some of the object's components. This promotes modularity and enhances code maintainability.

Inheritance is another key concept in object-oriented programming, allowing a class to inherit properties and methods from another class. In JavaScript, this is achieved using the `extends` keyword: javascript: class Animal {constructor(name) {this.name = name;} speak() {console.log(this.name + " makes a noise.");}}class Dog extends Animal {speak() {console.log(this.name + " barks.");}}let dog = new Dog("Rex");

Dog. Speak(); // Outputs: "Rex barks."

In this example, `Dog` inherits from `Animal` but overrides the `speak` method to provide specific behavior.

Python uses a similar approach with the `super` function to call the parent class's methods: Python: class Animal: def __init__(self, name): self.name = name: def speak(self): print(f"{self.name} makes a noise.")

class Dog(Animal): def speak(self):print(f"{self.name} barks."): dog = Dog("Rex"): dog.speak() # Outputs: "Rex barks."

Inheritance allows for code reuse and creates a more logical class hierarchy, promoting more transparent and manageable code structures.

Understanding objects, their creation, manipulation, methods, and properties is vital for effective programming in languages that support OOP. Objects encapsulate data and behavior, promoting modularity and code reuse. Methods allow objects to perform actions and interact with their properties, while properties store the object's state. Inheritance and the use of getters and setters provide powerful tools for creating flexible and maintainable code. These concepts are essential for building robust, scalable, and efficient software applications.

Working with Arrays

Working with arrays is a fundamental programming skill essential for managing and manipulating data collections. Arrays are ordered lists of elements that can be of any data type, and they are widely used in various programming languages such as JavaScript, Python, and Java. Understanding how to create arrays and utilize array methods is crucial for efficient data handling and manipulation.

Depending on the programming language, arrays can be created in several ways. In JavaScript, arrays can be created using array literals or the `Array` constructor. An array literal is the simplest way to create an array, using square brackets to enclose the elements:

Javascript let fruits = ["apple," "banana," "cherry"].

This creates an array named `fruits` containing three elements: "apple," "banana," and "cherry." Alternatively, the `Array` constructor can be used: javascript let numbers = new Array(1, 2, 3, 4, 5);

This creates an array named `numbers` with five elements. The constructor can also be used to create an array with a specified length: javascript: let empty Array = new Array (10).

This creates an array with ten undefined elements.

In Python, arrays are typically implemented using lists, similar to JavaScript arrays. A list can be created using square brackets:

Python: fruits = ["apple," "banana," "cherry"]

This creates a list named `fruits` with three elements. Python also provides the `list` constructor for creating lists: python

numbers = list((1, 2, 3, 4, 5)). This creates a list named `numbers` containing five elements.

Once arrays are created, various methods are available to manipulate their contents. JavaScript provides several built-in array methods for adding, removing, and modifying elements. The `push` method adds one or more elements to the end of an array: javascript: let fruits = ["apple," "banana"]; fruits. Push("cherry"); console.log(fruits); // ["apple," "banana," "cherry"].

The `pop` method removes the last element from an array and returns it: javascript: let fruits = ["apple," "banana," "cherry"]; let last fruit = fruits. Pop(); console.log(last fruit); // "cherry" console.log(fruits); // ["apple," "banana"]

Similarly, the `shift` method removes the first element from an array and returns it: javascript: let fruits = ["apple," "banana," "cherry"]; let first Fruit = fruits. Shift(); console.log(first Fruit); // "apple"

console.log(fruits); // ["banana," "cherry"]

The `unshift` method adds one or more elements to the beginning of an array: javascript: let fruits = ["banana," "cherry"]; fruits. Unshift("apple");

console.log(fruits); // ["apple," "banana," "cherry"]

Other useful array methods include `splice,` `slice,` and `concat.` The `splice` method changes the contents of an array by removing, replacing, or adding elements: javascript: let fruits = ["apple," "banana," "cherry"];

fruits. Splice (1, 1, "blueberry"); console.log(fruits); // ["apple," "blueberry," "cherry"].

In this example, `splice` removes one element at index one and adds "blueberry" at the same position. The `slice` method returns a shallow copy of a portion of an array: javascript: let fruits = ["apple," "banana," "cherry"]; let sliced fruits = fruits. Slice(1, 2); console.log(sliced fruits); // ["banana"]: The `concat` method merges two or more arrays: javascript

let fruits1 = ["apple," "banana"]; let fruits2 = ["cherry," "date"]; let all Fruits = fruits1.concat(fruits2); console.log(fruits); // ["apple," "banana," "cherry," "date"]

In Python, lists provide similar methods for manipulation. The `append` method adds an element to the end of a list: Python: fruits = ["apple," "banana"]: fruits. Append("cherry"): print(fruits) # ["apple," "banana," "cherry"]

The `pop` method removes and returns the last element of a list: Python: fruits = ["apple," "banana," "cherry"] last fruit = fruits. Pop() print(last fruit) # "cherry" print(fruits) # ["apple," "banana"]

The `insert` method adds an element at a specified position: Python

fruits = ["apple," "banana"] fruits. Insert(1, "cherry") print(fruits) # ["apple," "cherry," "banana"]

To remove an element by its value, the `remove` method is used: Python

fruits = ["apple," "banana," "cherry"] fruits. Remove("banana"): print(fruits) # ["apple," "cherry"]

Python lists also support slicing, which returns a new list containing a subset of elements. Python: fruits = ["apple," "banana," "cherry"] sliced fruits = fruits[1:2]print(sliced fruits) # ["banana"].

The `extend` method concatenates lists: Python: fruits1 = ["apple," "banana"] fruits2 = ["cherry," "date"] fruits1.extend(fruits2) print(fruits1) # ["apple," "banana," "cherry," "date"]

Working with arrays also involves understanding how to iterate over their elements. In JavaScript, the `for` loop, `forEach` method, and newer constructs like `map,` `filter,` and `reduce` provide flexible ways to process array elements. The `for` loop is straightforward: javascript

let fruits = ["apple," "banana," "cherry"]; for (let i = 0; i < fruits.length; i++){console.log(fruits[i]);}

The `forEach` method executes a provided function once for each array element: javascript: let fruits = ["apple," "banana," "cherry"]; fruits.forEach(function(fruit) {console.log(fruit); }).

The `map` method creates a new array with the results of calling a function on every element: javascript: let numbers = [1, 2, 3]; let doubled = numbers. Map(function(number) { return number $*^*$ 2;});console.log(doubled); // [2, 4, 6]

The `filter` method creates a new array with elements that pass a test: javascript: let numbers = [1, 2, 3, 4, 5]; let even Numbers = numbers.filter(function(number) {return number % 2 === 0; });console.log (even numbers); // [2, 4]

The `reduce` method executes a reducer function on each element, resulting in a single output value: javascript let numbers = [1, 2, 3, 4, 5]; let sum = numbers.reduce(function(total, number) {return total + number;}, 0);console.log(sum); // 15

Python provides similar iteration methods with list comprehensions and built-in functions like `map,` `filter,` and `reduce.` A basic `for` loop: Python fruits = ["apple," "banana," "cherry"] For fruit in fruits: print(fruit).

List comprehensions provide a concise way to create lists: Python numbers = [1, 2, 3] doubled = [number * 2 for number in numbers] print(doubled) # [2, 4, 6].

The `map` function applies a function to all items in an input list: Python: numbers = [1, 2, 3] doubled = list(map(lambda x: x * 2, numbers)) print(doubled) # [2, 4, 6].

The `filter` function creates a list of elements that satisfy a condition: python numbers = [1, 2, 3, 4, 5] even_numbers = list(filter(lambda x: x % 2 == 0, numbers))print(even_numbers) # [2, 4].

The `reduce` function applies a rolling computation to sequential pairs of values in a list: Python: from functools import reduce numbers = [1, 2, 3, 4, 5]: sum = reduce(lambda x, y: x + y, numbers) print(sum) # 15.

In summary, working with arrays involves creating, manipulating their elements using various methods, and iterating over their contents to perform operations. Arrays are versatile data structures that enable efficient storage and manipulation of data collections. Understanding how to use array methods like `push,` `pop,` `shift,` `unshift,` `splice,` `slice,` and `concat` in JavaScript and similar methods in Python allows developers to handle data effectively. Additionally, mastering iteration techniques and higher-order functions like `map,` `filter,` and `reduce` enhances the ability to process and transform array data. These skills are foundational for any programmer and are applicable across a wide range of applications and domains.

Advanced Array Methods

Advanced array methods like `map,` `filter,` and `reduce` are powerful tools in modern programming languages such as JavaScript and Python, offering efficient ways to manipulate arrays and process data. These methods are part of functional programming paradigms and are essential for writing clean, concise, and maintainable code.

The `map` method applies a provided function to each element in an array and returns a new array with the results. This allows for transforming each element in the original array without mutating it directly. For example, in JavaScript: javascript let numbers = [1, 2, 3, 4, 5]; let doubled = numbers. Map(function(number) { return number * 2.

}); console.log(doubled); // [2, 4, 6, 8, 10].

Here, `map` iterates through each element of `numbers,` applies the function `number * 2` to each component and returns a new array `doubled` with the transformed values.

In Python, `map` behaves similarly but returns an iterator that can be converted into a list: Python numbers = [1, 2, 3, 4, 5] doubled = list(map(lambda x: x * 2, numbers)) print(doubled) # [2, 4, 6, 8, 10].

The `map` function is proper for converting data types, applying mathematical operations, or formatting elements based on specific criteria across the entire array.

On the other hand, the `filter` method creates a new array with elements that pass a certain test defined by a provided function. It filters out elements that do not satisfy the condition. In JavaScript: javascript

let numbers = [1, 2, 3, 4, 5]; let evenNumbers = numbers.filter(function(number) { return number % 2 === 0;}); console.log(even numbers); // [2, 4]

Here, `filter` creates a new array of `even numbers` containing only the even numbers from the original array `numbers.`

In Python, `filter` similarly creates a new list: Python numbers = [1, 2, 3, 4, 5] even_numbers = list(filter(lambda x: x % 2 == 0, numbers)) print(even_numbers) # [2, 4].

The `filter` function helps select elements based on conditions such as even numbers, specific values, or more complex criteria defined by the provided function.

Finally, the `reduce` method applies a function to an accumulator and each element in the array (from left to right) to reduce it to a single value. It effectively reduces the array to a single value by iterating through each element and accumulating a result. In JavaScript: javascript let numbers = [1, 2, 3, 4, 5]; let sum = numbers.reduce(function(total, number) { return total + number;}, 0);console.log(sum); // 15

Here, `reduce` computes the sum of all elements in `numbers` starting with an initial value of `0` for `total.`

In Python, `reduce` is available in the `functions` module and must be imported: Python from functools import reduce numbers = [1, 2, 3, 4, 5]sum = reduce(lambda x, y: x + y, numbers, 0)print(sum) # 15

The `reduce` function is versatile and can be used for tasks such as computing totals, aggregating values, or performing cumulative operations on arrays.

These advanced array methods—` map,` `filter,` and `reduce`—promote functional programming principles by treating arrays as immutable data structures and emphasizing data transformation, selection, and aggregation. They provide concise and expressive ways to manipulate arrays without explicit loops or mutations, leading to more transparent and maintainable code. Understanding and mastering these methods are essential for developers aiming to write efficient, scalable, and readable code in both JavaScript and Python, and they form the backbone of functional programming practices that are increasingly valued in modern software development. By leveraging these methods effectively, developers can streamline data processing tasks, improve code quality, and enhance overall productivity in their programming endeavors.

CHAPTER VI

The Document Object Model (DOM)

Understanding the DOM

Web developers who want to create dynamic and interactive websites must comprehend the Document Object Model (DOM). A programming interface known as the Document Object Model (DOM) is offered by browsers and enables scripts to modify a document's style, structure, and content while it is being read. In essence, it acts as a web page representation, allowing applications to alter the document's content, style, and organization. Programmatic access to and manipulation of HTML and XML document elements is made possible via the Document Object Model (DOM), a hierarchical representation of a web document.

Every node in the tree-like structure that makes up the DOM reflects a different page section. These nodes could be text, attributes, or other items. For example, the element is the root node of the tree of an HTML document, and it has child nodes like `} and `}. These child nodes can also have child nodes of their own, such as {} and {<h1>}, creating a hierarchical structure that resembles the layout of an HTML document. It is simpler to navigate and work with the document because of its logical, hierarchical order made possible by the tree structure.

Programming languages like JavaScript, which is most frequently used for client-side scripting in web development, are usually used to access the DOM. Developers can dynamically build, edit, and remove components and attributes with JavaScript's many methods and properties for interacting with the DOM. The browser's implementation of the Document Object Model

(DOM) exposes a collection of objects and functions that can be used to change the document, facilitating this interaction.

Selecting elements is one of the basic responsibilities when working with the DOM. There are multiple ways to choose elements from the DOM in JavaScript. `getElementById}, `getElementsByClassName{, `getElem entsByTagName{, `querySelector}, and `querySelectorAll} are among the most frequently used methods. Each of these techniques has a distinct function and can be applied according to the demands of the current task. For example, `querySelectorAll` provides all elements that match a given CSS selector, whereas `getElementById} selects a single element with a certain ID.

After selecting the elements, working with them is simple. The `innerHTML` and `textContent` properties allow developers to alter an element's content. Complex HTML structures can be added to an element using the `innerHTML` property, which permits the insertion of HTML material within an element. Conversely, the text content of the designated node and its offspring can be set or returned using {textContent`. This approach is helpful when it is not desired for HTML tags to be included, as it removes them and only provides the text.

The DOM lets you change element styles and properties and manipulate content. The `getAttribute` and `setAttribute` methods allow you to access and modify attributes like {src,` `href{, and `alt}. For instance, choose the image element to alter an image's source and use `setAttribute('src,' 'newImage.jpg')} to update the image's source. Similarly, the {style} property allows CSS styles to be changed. Dynamic changes to the element's look are possible because this attribute gives access to the element's inline styles. Setting {element. style. For example, backgroundColor = 'blue'} causes the selected element's background color to change to blue.

The ability of the DOM to dynamically add and remove items is another powerful feature. Applications like forms and interactive lists that demand user participation will find this especially helpful. A new element can be made using the `createElement` method, after which it can be altered and added to the document. For instance, `document.createElement('div')} is used to create a new ` } element, which is then added to the DOM, its properties are set, and `append Child{ is used to append the element to the specified parent element. On the other hand, the {remove Child} method removes items by deleting a given child node from its parent.

Another essential component of the DOM is event management, which lets programmers make dynamic websites that react to user input. JavaScript can monitor and handle keystrokes, mouse movements, and clicks. Event handlers are often attached to elements using the `addEventListener` method. A button element must be chosen before utilizing `addEventListener('click,' function)} to add a click event. The function specifies what should happen when the event happens. This event-driven programming paradigm makes the development of interactive and responsive user interfaces possible.

Since the DOM is the foundation for how online pages are organized and altered, web developers must understand its nuances to create current websites. Developers can design rich, interactive web applications that improve user experience by taking advantage of the features provided by the DOM. The ability to dynamically update content, structure, and style through programmatic access and manipulation of the DOM enables developers to create apps that react in real time to user input and other stimuli.

The Document Object Model is a key idea in web development since it offers a programmatically accessible and manipulable organized representation of web documents. JavaScript allows developers to construct dynamic, interactive, and responsive web applications by handling events, changing elements, content, attributes, and styles, and adding and removing items on the fly. Any web developer who wants to create dynamic web pages that offer a rich and engaging user experience must have a firm grasp of the DOM.

Selecting DOM Elements

As a web developer, one of your most powerful tasks is selecting which DOM elements to use. This ability allows you to work with and modify a page's contents dynamically. The Document Object Model (DOM) is the structure of a web document, and JavaScript equips you with several methods to access these elements. `getElementById`, `getElementsByClassName`, `querySelector`, and `querySelectorAll` are some of the most frequently used methods. Each of these techniques, with their unique benefits and use cases, is a tool in your hands to shape a variety of web development scenarios.

One of the simplest and most popular methods for choosing DOM items is the {getElementById} function. Developers can access a single element by using its distinct ID attribute. The ID attribute in an HTML document needs to be unique. Therefore, two items cannot have the same ID. Because of its uniqueness, `getElementById} is an effective tool for clearly addressing individual elements. For instance, a developer can use `document.getElementById('buttonId')} to access a button assigned an ID and alter it on the page. If no such element exists, this function returns {null}. Otherwise, it returns the first element with the given ID. {getElementById} is a highly efficient selection method that performs faster than other methods because it directly targets an aspect.

However, to choose several items with the same class property, use the `getElementsByClassName` method. Unlike IDs, class names are not unique and can be applied to more than one entity. The output of this method is a live HTMLCollection, an object that resembles an array and contains every element with the given class name. For example, document. get Elements By Class Name('highlight')} can be used by a developer to style or alter all items with the class name "highlight." This technique is helpful when working with sets of items that must be handled consistently, such as applying a consistent style or attaching event listeners to numerous buttons. But because {getElementsByClassName} yields a live collection, modifications to the DOM are instantly reflected in the collection, which occasionally results in unexpected behavior if the DOM is heavily altered.

Because it enables CSS selectors to locate the first element that fits a given selection, `querySelector` is a more flexible and potent way to select DOM elements. With CSS selectors, you may target items according to various criteria, including IDs, class names, tag names, and attribute values, in a versatile and expressive manner. The selection of the first element with the class "item" that descends from a component with the ID "main" can be achieved, for instance, by using `document.querySelector('#main. item')}. `querySelector` is a beneficial tool for targeting elements in deeply nested structures or when precise combinations of attributes are needed because it may employ sophisticated selections. It is less valuable when numerous items must be chosen, as it only returns the first matched element.

`QuerySelectorAll` is the recommended approach for picking several elements based on a CSS selector. While it produces a static NodeList with all elements that match the supplied selector, it functions similarly to `querySelector.` Since this NodeList is not live, modifications to the DOM do not cause it to update instantly. Developers can use `document.querySelectorAll('#main. item')` to retrieve all elements with the class "item" within a component with the ID "main." Batch processing of elements is possible by utilizing regular array techniques to loop over the resulting NodeList. Because the selection remains the same unless it is specifically re-executed, the NodeList's static nature guarantees predictable behavior.

Every one of these approaches has benefits and is appropriate for a specific web development assignment. When it's necessary to swiftly and effectively retrieve a single, distinct element, `getElementById}` works perfectly. Due to its speed and simplicity, it is the preferred option for focusing on particular aspects without the need for intricate selectors. When managing groups of elements with the same class, `getElementsByClassName` is helpful since it enables developers to make changes consistently to several components. When real-time updates to the DOM are needed, its live nature can be beneficial, but it must be handled carefully to prevent unexpected results.

The most flexible selectors are `querySelector` and `querySelectorAll}`, which use CSS selectors' capabilities to target components according to various parameters. When only the first matching element is required, `querySelector` works flawlessly; however, `querySelectorAll` is essential when several elements must be chosen and handled simultaneously. Because the NodeList produced by `querySelectorAll}` is static, managing and manipulating selected components is more accessible, and consistent behavior is ensured.

In actual use, these techniques can be coupled to accomplish complex DOM modifications. To locate all child elements within a container with a particular class, a developer could, for instance, use `querySelectorAll}` after selecting the container element using `getElementById.` This combination makes it possible to target items precisely and effectively, enabling intricate interactions and dynamic page modifications.

Modern web development requires an understanding of these techniques and their efficient application. By giving developers, the means to work with the DOM, they facilitate the creation of dynamic and adaptable online applications. Proficiency in element selection techniques facilitates targeted and efficient manipulation of the Document Object Model (DOM), augmenting online applications' functionality and user experience. Developers can use the advantages of each approach to create dependable, adaptable solutions that satisfy the various requirements of the modern web environment.

Modifying DOM Elements

A key component of web development is modifying DOM (Document Object Model) elements, which enables programmers to dynamically alter a web page's content, styles, and structure without having to refresh it. The Document Object Model (DOM) serves as a programming interface for online documents, describing the page so that programs can alter its content, structure, and design. Having this capacity is essential for developing responsive and interactive web applications.

Changing the content of DOM components is one of the main ways to edit them. JavaScript, a scripting language frequently used in web development, can accomplish this. Developers use properties like `innerHTML,` `textContent,` or `innerText` to modify an element's content. The `innerHTML` attribute can enter HTML material inside an element. Take `document.getElementById("example"), for instance.innerHTML = "

New content ";} adds a new paragraph to the element's existing content and assigns it the id "example." Though effective, this technique should be used cautiously to prevent security flaws like cross-site scripting (XSS). Alternatively, you can set or retrieve an element's text content using `textContent` and `innerText,` which remove HTML tags. Adding plain text material is safer since these properties do not parse HTML.

One further crucial component of web development is altering the styles of DOM elements and content. An element's `style}` attribute can be used for this. Using the ' style ' property, developers can dynamically modify an element's CSS (Cascading Style Sheets) properties. For example, the text color of the element with the id "example" is changed to blue by `document.getElementById("example").style.color = "blue";`. Similarly, you may alter additional CSS attributes like `display}`, `fontSize}`, and `backgroundColor` to produce a dynamic and eye-catching user interface. Moreover, an element's CSS classes can be added, removed, or toggled using the {classList` property. Developers can modify the element's classes using `classList.add("new-class")`, `classList.remove("old-class")`, or `classList.toggle("active")`, enabling more intricate style changes through preset CSS rules.

Another essential function that makes dynamic page updates possible is the addition and removal of elements from the DOM. To add elements, developers can utilize `createElement,` `appendChild,` `insertBefore,` and `insertAdjacentHTML,` among other methods. A new element can be created using the `createElement` method, and `appendChild` can be used to append it to the DOM. `let new paragraph == document.createElement("p"); newParagraph.textContent

"This is a new paragraph."; document.getElementById("example").appendChild(new paragraph);}` is an example of how to add a new paragraph to a div. This code creates the new paragraph element, its text content is set, and it is appended as a child of the div with the id "example." More control over the positioning of new elements is available with the `insertBefore` method, which enables putting an element before a specified child of a parent element. Furthermore, `insertAdjacentHTML` provides an additional flexible option to add content by inserting HTML directly at specified places relative to an existing element.

The `removeChild` and `remove` methods can remove elements from the DOM. A reference to the parent and child elements that must be removed is needed for the `removeChild` method to work. For instance, to remove the child element from its parent, use the code {let parent = document.getElementById("example"); let child = document.getElementById("child-element"); parent.removeChild(child);}. On the other hand, the `remove` method {document.getElementById("child-element").remove();} can be called directly on the element that has to be removed. This technique streamlines the procedure by removing the need for an explicit reference to the parent element.

These ways of modifying DOM elements allow the development of dynamic web apps that react to events and user interactions. For example, DOM manipulation enables live search results, interactive content updates, and form validation. To execute functions in reaction to user activities like clicks, inputs, or mouse movements, event listeners are essential to this process. Developers can add and remove elements based on user interactions, trigger changes to content and style, and more by adding event listeners to elements.

Even though DOM modification is an effective tool, it must be utilized carefully to guarantee maintainability and optimal performance. Performance costs can arise from directly modifying the DOM, particularly when done frequently or extensively. The impacted portions of the page must be re-rendered by browsers, which may cause performance snags. Developers can lessen this by employing document fragments, which enable batch DOM updates and reduce reflows and repaints. Furthermore, developers can write more effective and manageable code thanks to abstractions and optimizations for DOM manipulation offered by contemporary JavaScript frameworks and libraries like React, Vue, and Angular.

When making modifications to the DOM, security considerations are also crucial. As was previously discussed, apps that use {innerHTML} may be vulnerable to XSS attacks if DOM content that is not trusted is introduced. To avoid this, developers should sanitize user input and insert plain text using safer ways, such as {textContent}. An additional degree of protection can be added by implementing Content Security Policy (CSP) headers, which limit the execution of dangerous scripts.

In conclusion, a key component of contemporary web development is the ability to alter DOM elements by adding, deleting, and changing their content and styling. These methods enable the development of responsive, dynamic, and interactive web applications. With the help of JavaScript and a thorough understanding of the DOM, developers can easily create complex user interfaces that react to user input. Power must be balanced with performance factors and security best practices to maintain web applications' speed, effectiveness, and security.

CHAPTER VII

Event Handling

Introduction to Events

A key idea in web development, events operate as a conduit between user input and the interactive replies that web apps provide. Developing dynamic, responsive, and captivating user experiences requires a thorough understanding of events. An event is any user-initiated interaction on a webpage, such as clicking a button, dragging the cursor over an element, or pushing a key. The system can also start events, such as when an animation ends, or a web page loads completely. Developers can create more interactive and user-friendly user interfaces for their web apps by utilizing events to specify how the programs should react to different interactions.

Various sorts of events are distinguished according to the type of interaction. The "click" event frequently occurs when users click on an element, usually a button, link, or other interactive component. Activities like submitting a form, switching to a different page, or changing content visibility depend on the click event. Adding event listeners—functions that run in reaction to an event—to elements is how click events are handled. JavaScript can be used, for example, to add a click event listener to a button that initiates a function that shows an alert or retrieves data from a server.

The "mouseover" event, which happens when a user moves the mouse pointer over an element, is another commonly used event type. By offering interactive feedback, such as highlighting a menu item, displaying tooltips, or starting animations, this event is frequently used to improve the user experience. The "mouseout" event, which happens when the mouse pointer departs an element, is the equivalent of the mouseover event. These events can produce dynamic hover effects that enhance a website's usability and aesthetic appeal. Developers frequently use these events to create interactive menus, picture galleries, and other components that change visually in response to user input.

Keyboard events are also essential for online applications—particularly those that depend on user input via forms or keyboard shortcuts. A keystroke on the keyboard causes the "key-down" event to be initiated, while releasing the key causes the "key-up" event. Additionally, when a key is depressed and held down, an event known as "keypress" occurs. These events are necessary for providing keyboard shortcuts, validating forms, and creating accessible web apps that allow keyboard input navigation. Developers may improve the accessibility and usability of their programs and make them more inclusive of users with varying requirements and preferences by registering and reacting to keyboard events.

In online applications that require user input, form events are essential. When a user submits a form, usually by clicking a submit button or hitting the Enter key, the "submit" event is triggered. By managing the submit event, developers can use JavaScript to manage the data and carry out tasks like data processing, form validation, and stopping the default behavior of a form submission. The "change" event, generated when the value of an input, select, or textarea element changes, is another significant form event. This event can be used to create interactive forms that react instantly to user input, validate forms in real time, and update content dynamically based on user input.

To control a web page's lifetime, the "load" event is essential. It happens when the page's dependent resources—like stylesheets and images—have finished loading. This event is especially crucial for initializing scripts to ensure that the DOM is entirely created before changing it. Developers frequently use the load event to start processes that require the entire page's content, like initializing plugins, configuring event listeners, and making layout changes. Similarly, the "DOMContentLoaded" event happens as soon as the first HTML document loads and is processed entirely—before stylesheets, images, and subframes are fully loaded. When scripts are executed as soon as the DOM is prepared, this event makes faster interactions and better performance possible.

With the increasing use of mobile devices and touch interfaces, touch events have become more significant. Among these events are "touchstart," "touchmove," and "touched," which are set off when a user touches, swipes, or raises the screen, respectively. With touch events, developers can design responsive and user-friendly mobile interfaces with touch-based interactions like pinch-to-zoom and swipe movements. Developers may accommodate diverse user behaviors and preferences by tailoring their programs to deliver a smooth and captivating user experience across desktop and mobile platforms by handling touch events.

Other noteworthy examples are the "focus" and "blur" event types associated with input components. The focus event occurs when an element becomes focused, usually due to a user clicking on an input field or using the keyboard to navigate. When an element loses focus—for example, when a user clicks outside an input field—the blur event is triggered. These events are critical for tasks like controlling the visual state of form elements, displaying or concealing helpful text, and validating input. Developers can construct forms that help users through the input process, give real-time feedback, and enhance overall form usability by handling focus and blur events.

Numerous other event kinds in web development have specific uses besides these popular ones. For instance, when the browser window is resized, the "resize" event is triggered, enabling developers to modify a page's design and styling dynamically. When a user scrolls the page, the "scroll" event is triggered, which makes it possible to implement features like lazy image loading, endless scrolling, and dynamic content updates based on the scroll position. When a user right-clicks on an element, a context menu usually opens. This is known as the "context menu" event. Through the handling of this event, developers can design unique context menus that enhance user engagement and offer more features.

To sum up, events are an essential component of web development that lets programmers design responsive and dynamic websites. Through comprehension and utilization of diverse event categories, including click, mouseover, keyboard, form, load, touch, focus, and others, programmers can construct apps that react instantly to user input, offering a smooth and captivating user interface. Modern web developers must be proficient in event handling to design dynamic, interactive interfaces that satisfy user expectations across various platforms and devices.

Adding Event Listeners

Adding event listeners to elements is a crucial technique in web development that allows developers to define specific behaviors in response to user actions. Event listeners are functions executed when a particular event occurs on a specified element. By attaching event listeners to elements, developers can create interactive and dynamic web applications that respond in real time to user inputs such as clicks, key presses, and mouse movements. This process involves selecting the target element and defining the event type and the callback function that handles the event. Understanding how to add listeners and manage event propagation effectively is essential for building sophisticated and user-friendly web applications.

To attach an event listener to an element, developers typically use JavaScript's `addEventListener` method. This method takes three arguments: the type of event to listen for, the callback function to execute when the event occurs, and an optional boolean value that specifies whether to use event capturing. The event type is a string that identifies the specific event, such as "click," "mouseover," "keydown," or "submit." The event handler's callback function contains the code that will run when the event is triggered. This function can either be an existing or anonymous function defined directly within the `addEventListener` call.

For example, to attach a click event listener to a button element, a developer might use the following code: javascript let button = document.getElementById('button); button. addEventListener('click', function() {alert('Button was clicked!');}).

In this example, the click event listener is attached to the button element with the ID "button." When the button clicks, the anonymous function defined within the `addEventListener` method is executed, displaying an alert message.

Event listeners can be added to various elements, including buttons, links, form inputs, and document or window objects. This flexibility allows developers to create interactive features like form validation, dynamic content updates, and custom user interactions. Additionally, multiple event listeners can be attached to a single element for different events or even for the same event type. Each event listener operates independently, allowing developers to define complex behaviors without interference.

Event propagation is a fundamental concept in event handling, describing how events travel through the DOM when triggered. There are two main phases of event propagation: event capturing and event bubbling. Understanding these phases is essential for managing events and ensuring the correct elements respond to user actions.

Event capturing, or the capture phase, occurs first in the event propagation process. During this phase, the event travels from the root of the DOM tree down to the target element. This means that the document object first captures the event and then travels through parent elements down to the component that triggered the event. By default, event listeners do not capture events in this phase unless explicitly specified. To enable capturing, the third argument of the `addEventListener` method must be set to `true.'

For example: javascript document. AddEventListener('click', function() {console.log('Document captured click event');}, true).

In this example, the click event listener is set to capture the event during the capturing phase. As a result, when a click event occurs anywhere in the document, the event listener on the document object will be triggered first, before any other event listeners on child elements.

After the capturing phase, the event reaches the target element, and the target phase begins. Any event listeners attached directly to the target element during this phase are executed. This phase is straightforward, as it involves the aspect that initially triggered the event.

Following the target phase is the event bubbling phase. In this phase, the event travels back up the DOM tree from the target element to the root, triggering any event listeners on parent elements. By default, event listeners are set to handle events during the bubbling phase, so event listeners are often triggered in an order that reflects the hierarchical structure of the DOM.

For example: javascript document. Add Event Listener('click', function(){console.log('Document bubbled click event');}).

In this example, the click event listener is set to handle the event during the bubbling phase. When a click event occurs on any element within the document, the event will bubble up to the document object, triggering this event listener after all other event listeners on child elements have been executed.

Event propagation allows for the implementation advanced event-handling techniques, such as event delegation. Event delegation leverages event bubbling to manage events more efficiently by attaching a single event listener to a parent element instead of multiple listeners to each child element. This is particularly useful for dynamically generated content, as it eliminates the need to reattach event listeners every time the DOM changes.

For example: javascript document get Element By Id('parent').addEventListener('click', function(event) {if (event. Target && event.target.matches('button.child')) {console.log('Child button clicked');}}).

A single-click event listener is attached to the parent element in this example. When any child button element is clicked, the event bubbles up to the parent, where the event listener checks if the target matches the specified selector. If so, the desired action is executed. This approach simplifies event management and improves performance, especially in applications with many interactive elements.

Managing event propagation effectively requires understanding how to stop events from continuing through the propagation phases. This can be achieved using methods like `event stop Propagation` and `event stop Immediate Propagation`. The `stop Propagation` method prevents the event from bubbling up or capturing down the DOM tree, while `stop Immediate Propagation` also prevents other listeners on the same element from being executed.

For example: javascript button Add Event Listener('click',function (event) event stop Propagation();console.log('Button click handled, propagation stopped');}).

In this example, the click event listener on the button element stops the event from propagating further up the DOM tree, ensuring that no parent elements' event listeners are triggered.

In conclusion, adding event listeners to elements is fundamental to creating interactive web applications. The `addEventListener` method allows developers to define how elements should respond to various events, enabling dynamic and responsive user interfaces. Understanding event propagation, including the capturing and bubbling phases, is essential for managing event handling effectively. By leveraging event delegation and controlling event propagation, developers can build sophisticated and efficient event-driven applications that provide a seamless user experience.

Creating Custom Events

Creating custom events in web development allows developers to define and dispatch their events, enabling a higher degree of interaction and communication within web applications. Custom events are beneficial for decoupling different parts of an application, facilitating the interaction between components, and enhancing the modularity and maintainability of the code. JavaScript provides a straightforward mechanism to create and dispatch custom events using the `CustomEvent` constructor and the `dispatchEvent` method.

Creating a custom event starts with the `CustomEvent` constructor, which allows developers to define a new event type with specific details. The `CustomEvent` constructor takes two arguments: the event's name and an optional configuration object. The event's name is a string that identifies the custom event, while the configuration object can include additional properties such as `detail,` `bubbles,` and `cancelable.` The `detail` property is fundamental as it allows developers to pass additional data with the event, which can be accessed by event listeners when the event is dispatched.

For example, to create a custom event named "user logged in" that carries user information, a developer might use the following code: javascript

let user event = new CustomEvent('user logged in,' {detail: {

username: 'john doe,' role: 'admin.'}, bubbles: true, cancelable: true}).

In this example, the `user event` custom event is created with a `detail` property containing the username and role of the user. The `bubbles` property is set to `true,` indicating that the event will propagate up the DOM tree, and the `cancelable` property is set to `true,` allowing the event to be canceled if necessary.

Once a custom event is created, it can be dispatched to the target element using the `dispatchEvent` method.

This method is called on the component that should be the source of the event, triggering any event listeners listening for the custom event on that element or its ancestors (if the event bubbles). Dispatching the custom event is as simple as calling `dispatchEvent` with the custom event object: javascript document.getElementById('login button).dispatchEvent(user event);

In this example, the custom `userEvent` is dispatched from the element with the ID "loginButton". Any event listeners attached to this element or its ancestors listening for the "user logged in" event will be triggered, and they can access the event details through the event object passed to the listener.

Event listeners for custom events are defined in the same way as listeners for standard events, using the `addEventListener` method. Developers can attach listeners to specific elements or to the document object to handle custom events at a higher level. When the custom event is dispatched, the listener receives an event object containing the event's type, details, and other properties.

For example, to handle the "user logged in" custom event and access the user information, a developer might use the following code:

Javascript document add Event Listener ('userLoggedIn', function(event) {console.log(`User logged in: ${event.detail.username} with role ${event.detail.role}

In this example, an event listener is attached to the document object for the "user logged in" event. When the event is dispatched, the listener logs the username and role of the logged-in user, demonstrating how the additional data passed with the event can be accessed and used.

Custom events can also be canceled if they are defined as cancelable. To cancel a custom event, the event listener can call the `preventDefault` method on the event object. This can be useful for preventing default actions or indicating that a particular operation should not proceed.

For example, a developer might use the following code:
javascript

document to cancel a custom event Add Event Listener('userLoggedIn', function(event){if (event.detail.role !== 'admin') {

event.preventDefault();Console.log('Only admin users are allowed to log in'); }});letloginSuccess=document.getElementById('login button).dispatchEvent(user event);if (!login success) {console.log('Login event was canceled');}

In this example, the event listener checks the user's role and cancels the event if the user is not an admin. The `dispatchEvent` method returns a boolean value indicating whether the event was canceled, allowing the code to respond accordingly.

Custom events are also valuable in modern web development frameworks and libraries, where they can facilitate communication between components. For example, in a component-based architecture, one component might dispatch a custom event to notify other components of a state change or user action. This approach promotes loose coupling between components, making the codebase more modular and easier to maintain.

Additionally, custom events can be used to create complex interactions and workflows within an application. By defining a series of custom events and event listeners, developers can orchestrate intricate sequences of actions, such as form validation steps, multi-step processes, or real-time data updates. Custom events enable the creation of flexible and reusable components that can be easily integrated and extended.

In summary, creating and dispatching custom events in JavaScript provides developers with a powerful tool for enhancing the interactivity and modularity of web applications. The `CustomEvent` constructor and `dispatchEvent` methods define and trigger custom events, while event listeners handle these events like standard events. Custom events facilitate communication between different parts of an application, promote loose coupling, and enable the creation of complex interactions and workflows. By leveraging custom events, developers can build more dynamic, responsive, and maintainable web applications that respond to user actions and system changes flexibly and efficiently.

CHAPTER VIII

Asynchronous JavaScript

Introduction to Asynchronous Programming

Asynchronous programming is a paradigm in computer science that allows for executing non-blocking operations, enabling programs to remain responsive while waiting for long-running tasks to complete. This approach contrasts with synchronous programming, where operations are performed sequentially, and each task must be completed before the next one begins. Understanding the differences between synchronous and asynchronous code and the mechanisms that facilitate asynchronous behavior, such as the event loop, is essential for modern web development and efficiently handling tasks like I/O operations, network requests, and user interactions.

In synchronous programming, code execution happens line by line, and each operation must wait for the previous one to finish before it can start. This model is simple and intuitive but can lead to inefficiencies, mainly when dealing with tasks that involve waiting, such as reading from a file or making an HTTP request. For example, in a synchronous context, if a program needs to fetch data from a remote server, it will send the request and block all further execution until the response is received. During this waiting period, the program is unresponsive, which can degrade the user experience, especially in interactive applications.

On the other hand, asynchronous programming allows multiple operations to be initiated without waiting for previous ones to complete. This is achieved through mechanisms that enable tasks to run concurrently, such as callbacks, promises, and async/await syntax in

JavaScript. Using asynchronous techniques, a program can start a long-running task and continue executing other operations while waiting for the task to finish. Once the task is completed, a callback function or promise handler can be invoked to process the result, ensuring the program remains responsive and efficient.

The event loop is a central component of asynchronous programming in JavaScript, providing the runtime mechanism that enables non-blocking behavior. The event loop continually monitors the call stack and the message queue, coordinating the execution of code, event handlers, and other tasks. When a program runs, function calls are placed on the call stack, and the event loop processes them individually. If an asynchronous operation is encountered, such as a setTimeout or a network request, it is offloaded to the browser's web APIs, allowing the call stack to continue processing other tasks.

Once the asynchronous operation completes, the associated callback function is placed in the message queue. The event loop then checks if the call stack is empty; if it is, it takes the first callback from the message queue and pushes it onto the call stack, where it gets executed. This cycle ensures that asynchronous operations do not block the main thread, allowing the program to handle multiple tasks concurrently and remain responsive.

To illustrate the difference between synchronous and asynchronous code, consider the following examples. In a synchronous scenario, reading a file and logging its contents might look like this: javascript const fs = require('fs'); const data = fs.readFileSync('file. txt', 'utf8'); console.log(data); console.log('File read complete').

In this example, the call to `fs.readFileSync` blocks the execution until the file is completely read. The program can only proceed to the following line once this operation finishes, which can be inefficient if the file is large, or the I/O operation is slow.

In contrast, an asynchronous version of the same operation using callbacks would look like this: javascript const fs = require('fs'); fs.readFile('file. txt', 'utf8', (err, data) => { if (err) throw err; console.log(data);}); console. log('File read initiated').

Here, `fs.readFile` is used instead of `fs.readFileSync`. The `fs.readFile` function initiates the file read operation and immediately returns control to the next line of code, allowing `console. Log ('File read initiated')` to execute without waiting for the file read to complete. Once the file is read, the callback function is called with the file's content, ensuring that the program can continue executing other tasks.

Promises to provide a more elegant way to handle asynchronous operations, avoiding the so-called "callback hell" caused by nested callbacks. A promise represents a value that may be available now, in the future, or never. It has three states: pending, fulfilled, and rejected. A promise-based version of the file read operation looks like this: javascript const fs = require('fs').promises; fs.readFile('file.txt', 'utf8') .then(data => {console.log(data);}) .catch(err => { console.error(err); });console.log('File read initiated').

In this example, `fs.readFile` returns a promise that, when resolved, provides the file content. The `then` method handles the fulfilled state, and the `catch` method handles any errors. This approach is more readable and maintainable compared to nested callbacks.

The introduction of async/await syntax in JavaScript has further simplified asynchronous programming by allowing developers to write asynchronous code that looks synchronous. The `async` keyword defines an asynchronous function, and the `await` keyword pauses the function's execution until the promise is resolved. This can be seen in the following example: javascript

```javascript
const fs = require('fs').promises; async function readFile() { try { const data = await fs.readFile('file.txt', 'utf8'); console.log(data);} catch (err) { console.error(err);} readFile(); Console.log('File read initiated');
```

The `readFile` function is marked asynchronous with the `async` keyword in this example. The `await` keyword pauses the execution until the promise returned by `fs.readFile` is resolved, making the code appear synchronous while still non-blocking.

The event loop plays a crucial role in managing the execution of asynchronous code. It ensures the JavaScript runtime can handle multiple tasks concurrently without blocking the main thread. This capability is vital for maintaining the performance and responsiveness of web applications, particularly those that involve user interactions, I/O operations, and network requests.

In summary, asynchronous programming enables developers to write efficient and responsive code by allowing multiple operations to run concurrently. Synchronous code executes sequentially, blocking subsequent operations until the current one completes, which can lead to inefficiencies. Asynchronous code, facilitated by callbacks, promises, and async/await syntax, allows programs to initiate long-running tasks and continue executing other operations while waiting for these tasks to be completed. The event loop is the mechanism that orchestrates this non-blocking behavior, managing the call stack and message queue to ensure that asynchronous operations do not hinder the responsiveness of the application. Understanding these concepts is essential for modern web development, enabling the creation of interactive and performant applications.

Working with Callbacks

Callbacks are a fundamental concept in asynchronous programming, particularly in JavaScript. They allow functions to be passed as arguments to other functions, which can then execute these functions later. This mechanism is essential for handling asynchronous operations such as reading files, making HTTP requests, and interacting with databases. Understanding how to define and use callbacks effectively is crucial for writing efficient and maintainable code. However, improper use of callbacks can lead to what is known as "callback hell," where nested callbacks make the code difficult to read and maintain.

To define and use callbacks, one must first understand a callback function. A callback function is simply a function that is passed as an argument to another function and is intended to be called after some operation is completed. For example, consider a simple asynchronous function that reads a file and then calls a callback function with the file's content: javascript const fs = require('fs'); function readFileAsync(filePath, callback) {fs.readFile(filePath, 'utf8', (err, data) => {if (err) { return callback(err);} callback(null, data);}).

In this example, `readFileAsync` is an asynchronous function that takes a file path and a callback function as arguments. The `fs.readFile` method reads the file asynchronously. Once the file is read, the callback function is called with either an error (if one occurred) or the file data. To use this function, you would pass it a callback function to handle the result: javascript readFileAsync('file. txt', (err, data) => { if (err) { return console. error('Error reading file:,' err);} console. log('File content:,' data);});

This demonstrates the basic pattern of defining and using callbacks in asynchronous operations. The callback function provides a way to handle the result of an asynchronous operation once it completes.

However, as the complexity of asynchronous operations increases, callbacks can become deeply nested, leading to callback hell. Callback hell, also known as the pyramid of doom, occurs when multiple asynchronous operations are chained together, each requiring a callback function. This results in code that is hard to read and maintain due to the nesting of callback functions. Here is an example illustrating callback hell: javascript function first operation(callback) {

setTimeout(() => {console.log('First operation complete').

callback(null, 'Result of first operation'); }, 1000);}.

function second operation(result from first, callback) {setTimeout(() => { console.log('Second operation complete'); callback(null, 'Result of second operation');}, 1000);} function third operation(resultFromSecond, callback) { setTimeout(() => {console.log('Third operation complete'); callback(null, 'Result of third operation');}, 1000);} first operation((err, result1) => { if (err) {return console.error(err);

second operation(result1, (err, result2) => {if (err) {return console.error(err);

third operation(result2, (err, result3)

if (err) return console.error(err);Console.log('Final result:', result3);

In this example, three asynchronous operations are performed in sequence, each dependent on the previous one. The result is a series of nested callbacks, making the code difficult to follow and maintain. Callback hell affects readability and increases the risk of errors, such as forgetting to handle the mistakes or inadvertently introducing logical bugs.

To mitigate callback hell, several strategies can be employed. One common approach is modularizing the code by breaking it into smaller, reusable functions. This can reduce nesting and make the code more readable. Additionally, JavaScript offers alternative asynchronous programming techniques, such as promises and the async/await syntax, which provide more elegant ways to handle asynchronous operations.

Promises offer a cleaner way to handle asynchronous operations and avoid callback hell. A promise represents a value that may be available now, in the future, or never. Promises have three states: pending, fulfilled, and rejected. They provide methods like `then,` `catch,` and `finally` to handle the result of asynchronous operations. Here is an example using promises to refactor the previous callback hell example: javascript function first operation() { return new Promise ((resolve, reject) => { setTimeout(() => { console. log('First operation complete'); resolve('Result of first operation');}, 1000); });}

function second operation(result from first) { return new Promise((resolve, reject) => { setTimeout(() => { console.log('Second operation complete'); resolve('Result of second operation');}, 1000);});}

function third operation(resultFromSecond) { return new Promise((resolve, reject) => {setTimeout(() => { console.log('Third operation complete'); resolve('Result of third operation');}, 1000);

first Operation

then(result1 => second operation(result1))

then(result2 => third operation(result2))

then(result3 => { console.log('Final result:', result3);.catch(err => {console.error(err);

In this example, each asynchronous operation returns a promise. The `then` method combines the operations, ensuring that each operation waits for the previous one to complete. The `catch` method handles any errors that occur during the process. This approach is much more readable and maintainable compared to nested callbacks.

The introduction of the async/await syntax in JavaScript further simplifies asynchronous programming by allowing developers to write asynchronous code that looks synchronous. The `async` keyword defines an asynchronous function, and the `await` keyword pauses the function's execution until the Promise is resolved. Here is the same example using async/await:

javascript async function performs operations

const result1 = await first operation().

const result2 = await second operation(result1).

const result3 = await third operation(result2).

console.log('Final result:', result3);} catch (err) {console.error(err);}}perform Operations().

In this example, the `perform Operations` function is defined as asynchronous using the `async` keyword. The `await` keyword pauses the function's execution until each Promise is resolved, making the code much easier to understand. The `try/catch` block is used to handle any errors that may occur.

In conclusion, callbacks are a fundamental aspect of asynchronous programming in JavaScript, enabling functions to be executed after completing asynchronous operations. While callbacks are powerful, they can lead to callback hell when used extensively, resulting in profoundly nested and hard-to-maintain code. To mitigate this issue, developers can modularize their code, use promises, or leverage the async/await syntax. Promises to provide a cleaner way to handle asynchronous operations by avoiding nested callbacks, while async/await allows developers to write asynchronous code that appears synchronous, improving readability and maintainability. Understanding and effectively managing callbacks and their alternatives is crucial for building efficient, responsive, and maintainable web applications.

Promises and Async/Await

Promises and JavaScript's async/await syntax are pivotal tools for managing asynchronous operations, offering cleaner, more readable, and maintainable alternatives to traditional callback-based approaches. Understanding how to create and use promises and leverage the async/await syntax is essential for modern JavaScript development, mainly when dealing with network requests, file I/O, and timers.

A promise in JavaScript represents a value that may be available now, in the future, or never. It is a placeholder for an asynchronous operation's eventual success or failure. Promises to have three states: pending, fulfilled, and rejected. A promise is created using the `Promise` constructor, which takes a function as an argument. This function, often called the executor, has two parameters: `resolve` and `reject.` `resolve` is when the operation is booming, and `Reject` is when the operation fails.

In this example, `fetchData` returns a promise. The executor function uses `setTimeout` to simulate an asynchronous operation. After one second, the promise is either resolved with a success message or rejected with an error message.

You can use this promise to chain the `then` and `catch` methods. The `then` method is called when the promise is fulfilled, and the `catch` method handles any errors if the promise is rejected:

This approach allows handling asynchronous operations in a more readable manner compared to deeply nested callbacks. Each `then` call can return a new promise, enabling chaining multiple asynchronous operations in a sequence.

However, promises can still lead to somewhat verbose and less intuitive code when dealing with complex sequences of asynchronous operations. This is where the async/await syntax comes in, offering a more concise and readable way to work with promises.

The async/await syntax is built on top of promises. An `async` function always returns a promise, and within this function, you can use the `await` keyword to pause the function's execution until a promise is resolved. This allows writing asynchronous code that looks and behaves more like synchronous code.

In this example, `fetchDataAsync` is declared an `async` function. Inside this function, `await fetchData()` pauses the execution until `fetchData` is resolved. If `fetch data` is fulfilled, the result is assigned to `data,` and if rejected, the error is caught in the `catch` block. This approach significantly enhances the readability and maintainability of the code by avoiding promise chaining and nested callbacks.

The true power of async/await becomes apparent when handling multiple asynchronous operations. For example, consider a scenario where you need to fetch user data and then fetch additional data based on the user information:

In this scenario, `fetchUser` and `fetchUserDetails` are asynchronous functions that return promises. Using async/await in `fetchUserData,` the operations are performed sequentially, but the code remains clean and easy to understand. The `await` keyword ensures the function waits for each promise to resolve before moving on to the next operation.

Async/await also simplifies error handling. In promise chaining, each `then` call can potentially have its own `catch,` leading to fragmented error handling logic. With async/await, you can use a single `try/catch` block to handle errors, providing a unified approach to error management.

Furthermore, async/await is highly beneficial when dealing with loops and conditional statements involving asynchronous operations.

Here, `processes` iterates over an array and processes each item asynchronously. The `await` keyword ensures that each item is processed one after the other, maintaining a straightforward control flow.

In conclusion, promises and the async/await syntax are essential tools for managing asynchronous operations in JavaScript. Promises can handle asynchronous operations more cleanly than traditional callbacks by avoiding profoundly nested code and allowing chaining. However, promises can still be somewhat cumbersome, especially when dealing with complex sequences of asynchronous tasks. The async/await syntax builds on promises, enabling developers to write asynchronous code that looks and behaves like synchronous code. This significantly improves readability, maintainability, and error handling. Understanding and effectively utilizing promises and async/await is crucial for modern JavaScript development, leading to more efficient and responsive applications.

CHAPTER XI

Working with APIs

Understanding APIs

An Application Programming Interface, commonly known as an API, is a powerful tool that allows different software applications to communicate and interact. It's like a universal translator, enabling one piece of software to access and use the services and functionalities of another, often a web service or a server. This can involve requesting data, submitting data for processing, or executing specific actions remotely. APIs are the backbone of modern software development, making it easier to connect different systems and use existing functionalities without needing to understand their internal workings.

APIs come in various types, each tailored to different use cases and requirements. One of the most prevalent types is Representational State Transfer (REST) APIs. REST APIs adhere to architectural principles that govern how resources are defined and addressed over the web. They typically use standard HTTP methods like GET, POST, PUT, and DELETE to perform CRUD (Create, Read, Update, Delete) operations on resources. REST APIs use structured data formats such as JSON or XML to exchange information between clients and servers, making them versatile and widely adopted for building web APIs.

In contrast to REST, GraphQL has gained popularity as a more flexible and efficient alternative for querying and manipulating data. GraphQL is a query language for APIs and a runtime for executing those queries with existing data. Unlike REST, which exposes multiple endpoints that return fixed data structures, GraphQL APIs allow clients to request precisely the data they need, and no more, in a single query. This reduces over-fetching and under-fetching of data, making GraphQL particularly suited for applications where efficient data fetching and real-time updates are essential, such as social media platforms and data-intensive applications.

Beyond REST and GraphQL, other specialized types of APIs cater to specific functionalities and domains. For instance, SOAP (Simple Object Access Protocol) APIs provide a protocol for exchanging structured information using XML over HTTP or other transport protocols. SOAP APIs have been prevalent in enterprise applications for a long time due to their strict standards for message formats and protocols. Still, their complexity and verbosity have led to a decline in popularity in favor of simpler alternatives like REST and GraphQL.

Another notable type is Webhooks, which enable servers to send real-time notifications or events to other systems as they happen rather than requiring the systems to poll for updates continuously. Webhooks are commonly used for integrating services that need to react to events promptly, such as triggering notifications, updating databases, or initiating workflows based on external actions.

Moreover, there are APIs designed for specific industries or purposes, such as financial APIs for accessing banking services, social media APIs for integrating with platforms like Twitter or Facebook, and geolocation APIs for retrieving location-based data. These specialized APIs give developers access to domain-specific functionalities and data, empowering them to create more feature-rich and integrated applications. For instance, a financial API could be used to develop a mobile banking app, while a social media API could be used to integrate a chat feature into a website.

The role of APIs extends beyond enabling communication between different software applications. They also serve as building blocks for creating new services, fostering innovation by allowing developers to combine functionalities from multiple sources into cohesive applications. APIs are pivotal in microservices architecture, where applications comprise loosely coupled, independently deployable services communicating through APIs. This approach enhances scalability, flexibility, and maintainability by decoupling different components of an application and allowing them to evolve independently.

As the digital landscape continues to evolve, APIs remain essential tools for unlocking the potential of data and services across diverse platforms and devices. Whether through RESTful architectures, GraphQL's flexible querying capabilities, or specialized interfaces for specific domains, APIs empower developers to build interconnected, data-driven applications that meet the demands of modern users and businesses. Understanding the types and capabilities of APIs is fundamental for developers aiming to leverage their full potential and create innovative solutions that drive the future of software development.

Fetch API

The Fetch API is a modern interface that allows developers to make HTTP requests and handle responses in web applications. It provides a more robust and flexible feature set than the older XMLHttpRequest, making it the preferred choice for working with network requests in JavaScript. Using the Fetch API, developers can retrieve resources from servers, send data, and handle both responses and errors in a streamlined manner. This section explores the fundamentals of making HTTP requests with the Fetch API, handling responses, and managing mistakes effectively.

At its core, the Fetch API is based on the concept of promises, which simplifies the process of handling asynchronous operations. A typical fetch request involves calling the fetch function with a URL and then using the .then and .catch methods to handle the response and any possible errors. Here's a basic example of making a GET request using the Fetch API: javascript fetch('https://api.example.com/data') then(response => response.json()) then(data => console.log(data)) catch(Error => console. Error ('Error:,' Error));

In this example, the fetch function is called with the resource URL. The first .then method processes the response, converting it from JSON format into a JavaScript object. The second .then method handles the data received from the response, and the .catch method catches and logs any errors that occur during the request. This simple structure makes the Fetch API easy to use and understand, even for developers new to JavaScript.

The Fetch API supports various HTTP methods, including GET, POST, PUT, DELETE, and more. To request with a method other than GET, developers can pass an options object as the second parameter to the fetch function. For example, to make a POST request, you can use the following code: javascript fetch('https://api.example.com/data,' { method: 'POST,' headers: { Content-Type': 'application/json'}, body: JSON.stringify({ key: 'value' then(response => response. json())then(data console.log(data)) catch(error => console.error('Error:', error));

In this example, the options object specifies the HTTP method as POST, sets the Content-Type header to indicate that the request body contains JSON data, and includes a body property with the JSON stringified payload. This structure allows developers to customize their requests to meet specific requirements, such as sending form data, updating resources, or deleting items from a server.

Handling responses with the Fetch API involves checking the response's status to ensure it was successful. A response is considered successful if the status code is in the range of 200-299. If the response is unsuccessful, the fetch promise is not rejected automatically, so developers must explicitly handle non-successful statuses. Here's an example of how to handle different response statuses: javascript fetch('https://api.example.com/data') then(response => { if (!response. ok) { throw new Error(`HTTP error! status: ${response.status}`);} return response.json(); then(data => console.log(data)) catch(error => console.error('Error:', error)).

In this code, the response. Ok property is checked to determine if the response was successful. If the response is not ok, an error is thrown with the status code. This Error is then caught by the .catch method, allowing developers to handle it appropriately.

Error handling is a crucial aspect of working with the Fetch API, as network requests can fail for various reasons, such as network issues, server errors, or incorrect URLs. To manage these errors effectively, developers can use the .catch method to catch any exceptions thrown during the request and response process. Additionally, providing meaningful error messages to users and implementing retry logic or fallback mechanisms when appropriate is essential.

For instance, handling network errors and providing user feedback can be implemented as follows: javascript

fetch('https://api.example.com/data') then(response => { if (!response. ok) { throw new Error (`HTTP error! status: ${response. status}`);} return response.json(); }) then(data => console.log(data)) catch(Error => { if (Error. Message === 'Failed to fetch') {console.error('Network error. Please check your internet connection.');} else { console.error('Error:', error.message);

In this example, the .catch method checks if the error message is 'Failed to fetch,' which indicates a network issue. If so, a specific message is logged to inform the user about the network problem. Otherwise, the generic error message is logged.

The Fetch API also supports more advanced features like handling request timeouts, streaming responses, and working with non-JSON data formats. For example, to implement a timeout for a fetch request, developers can use the Abort Controller to cancel the request if it takes too long: javascript const controller = new Abort Controller();

const timeout = setTimeout(() => controller. Abort(), 5000);

fetch('https://api.example.com/data', { signal: controller. Signal }) then(response => { clear Timeout(timeout); if (!response. ok) { throw new Error(`HTTP error! status: ${response.status}`);}

return response.json();}) then(data => console.log(data)) catch(error => { if (error.name === 'AbortError') { console.error('Request timed out'); } else {console.error('Error:', error);

In this code, the Abort Controller creates a signal that can be passed to the fetch request. A timeout is set using setTimeout, and if the request takes longer than the specified time (5000 milliseconds in this case), the controller. Abort() method is called to cancel the request. The .catch method then checks if the Error is an AbortError and logs a specific message for the timeout.

The Fetch API also allows handling streaming responses, which is useful for working with large datasets or media files that need to be processed incrementally. For example, to handle a streaming response, developers can use the Readable Stream interface: javascript

```javascript
fetch('https://api.example.com/large-file') then(response => { const reader = response. Body get Reader(); const decoder = new Text Decoder(); let result = ''; function read() { reader. Read().then(({ done, value }) => { if (done) { console.log('Stream complete'); console.log(result); return;} result += decoder. Decode(value, { stream: true }); read(); catch(error => console.error('Error:', error));
```

In this example, the response body is accessed as a Readable Stream, and a reader is created to read the stream incrementally. The text Decoder decodes the streamed data as text, and the read function reads chunks of data until the stream is complete. This approach allows developers to handle significant responses efficiently without blocking the main thread.

Growing your business on the web and mobile relies on communicating, integrating, and connecting your products and services with different software programs. Application programming interfaces (APIs) are the key to doing this well—with the most flexibility, simplicity, safety, and control.

APIs are becoming the digital connective tissue of modern organizations, adding new capabilities to everything from their operations and products to their partnership strategies. It's no longer a stretch to say that most organizations don't ask whether to engage in API programs but how to do so.

An API gateway is an API management tool between a client and a collection of backend services.

An API gateway acts as a reverse proxy to accept all application programming interface (API) calls, aggregate the services required to fulfill them and return the appropriate result.

API architecture is usually explained in terms of client and server. The application sending the request is called the client, and the application sending the response is called the server. So, in the weather example, the bureau's weather database is the server, and the mobile app is the client.

There are four different ways that APIs can work depending on when and why they were created.

SOAP APIs : These APIs use Simple Object Access Protocol. Client and server exchange messages using XML. This is a less flexible API that was more popular in the past.

RPC APIs: These APIs are called Remote Procedure Calls. The client completes a function (or procedure) on the server, and the server sends the output back to the client. WebSocket API is another modern web API development that uses JSON objects to pass data. A WebSocket API supports two-way communication between client apps and the server. The server can send callback messages to connected clients, making it more efficient than REST API.

REST APIs: These are the most popular and flexible APIs found on the web today. The client sends requests to the server as data. The server uses this client input to start internal functions and returns output data back to the client. Let's look at REST APIs in more detail below.

Working with non-JSON data formats, such as plain text, Blob, or Form Data, is straightforward with the Fetch API. For example, to handle a plain text response, developers can use the response. Text() method: javascript fetch('https://api.example.com/text-data') then(response => { if (!response. ok) { throw new Error(`HTTP error! status: ${response.status}`); return response. Text(); then(data => console.log(data)) catch(error => console.error('Error:', error));

In this code, the response. Text() method is used to read the response as plain text, and the resulting text is logged to the console. This method works with endpoints that return text-based data, such as HTML or plain text files.

In conclusion, the Fetch API is a powerful and flexible tool for making HTTP requests and handling responses in JavaScript. It simplifies working with network requests by providing a modern, promise-based interface. Developers can build robust and reliable web applications by understanding how to create and customize requests, handle responses, and manage errors effectively. Advanced features, such as handling timeouts, streaming responses, and working with different data formats, further enhance the capabilities of the Fetch API, making it an essential tool for modern web development. By mastering the Fetch API, developers can ensure that their applications communicate with servers efficiently and handle network interactions gracefully, providing a smooth and seamless user experience

Parsing JSON Data

Parsing JSON (JavaScript Object Notation) data and converting between JSON and JavaScript objects is a fundamental skill in web development and modern programming. JSON is a lightweight data-interchange format that is easy for humans to read and write and for machines to parse and generate. It primarily transmits data between a server and a web application as text. Understanding how to work with JSON effectively allows developers to handle data exchange seamlessly and efficiently.

JSON data is a collection of name/value pairs where the name is a string, and the value can be a string, number, object, array, true, false, or null. This structure makes JSON an ideal format for presenting complex data structures concisely and readably. The syntax of JSON is derived from JavaScript object notation, but JSON is language-independent and supported by many programming environments and libraries.

When working with JSON data in JavaScript, one of the primary tasks is to parse JSON strings into JavaScript objects. This is typically done using the `JSON.parse()` method. This method transforms a JSON-formatted string into a corresponding JavaScript object. For example, given a JSON string `let jsonString = '{"name": "John," "age":30, "city": "New York"}';,` the code `let jsonObj = JSON.parse(jsonString);` will convert this string into a JavaScript object with properties `name,` `age,` and `city.` This object can then be manipulated using standard JavaScript methods and properties.

Conversely, converting a JavaScript object to a JSON string is achieved using the `JSON.stringify()` method. This method converts a JavaScript object into a JSON-formatted string suitable for transmission or storage. For instance, `let jsonString = JSON.stringify(jsonObj);` where `jsonObj` is a JavaScript object, will produce a JSON string representing the object. This string can be sent to a server, stored in a file, or used in any context where JSON is needed.

A common use case for JSON parsing and stringifying is in web applications that communicate with APIs. APIs (Application Programming Interfaces) often return data in JSON format, which needs to be parsed into JavaScript objects for use within the application. For example, when fetching user data from a server, a typical workflow involves making an HTTP request using `fetch(),` parsing the JSON response, and then using the resulting JavaScript object in the application. The code might look like this: javascript fetch('https://api.example.com/user').then(response => response.json()) .then(data => { console.log(data); // Use the data here: catch(error => console.error('Error fetching data:', error));

In this example, `fetch()` makes an HTTP request to the specified URL. The `response.json()` method parses the JSON data from the response into a JavaScript object, which is then logged to the console or used in the application.

In addition to straightforward data exchange, JSON parsing and stringifying can be used for more complex tasks, such as deep cloning of objects, handling nested structures, and managing optional and dynamic data. Deep cloning involves creating a new object that is a deep copy of an existing object, including all nested objects. This can be achieved using `JSON.parse(JSON.stringify(obj)),` where `obj` is the original object. This technique ensures that the new object is entirely separate from the original, with no shared references.

Handling nested structures in JSON requires careful parsing and manipulation of the resulting JavaScript objects. Consider a JSON object representing a user with an address field that is itself an object: javascript

let jsonString = '{"name": "John," "age":30, "address": {"street": "123 Main St", "city": "New York"}}'; let user = JSON.parse(jsonString).

console.log(user.address.city); // Outputs: New York

In this example, the `address` field is parsed into a nested JavaScript object, allowing access to its properties using dot notation. This nesting capability makes JSON a powerful format for representing complex data hierarchies.

Managing optional and dynamic data in JSON involves checking for the presence of fields and handling them appropriately in JavaScript. For instance, when parsing a JSON object that may or may not include certain properties, developers should use conditional statements to check for their existence before accessing them. This prevents runtime errors and ensures robust code. Example: javascript let jsonString = '{"name": "John," "age":30}'; let user = JSON.parse(jsonString); if (user.address) {

console.log(user.address.city); } else { console.log("Address not provided");}`

Here, the code checks if the `address` property exists before attempting to access its `city` property, providing a fallback message if it does not.

Working with JSON in JavaScript also involves appropriately understanding and handling various data types. JSON supports strings, numbers, objects, arrays, booleans, and null, each of which needs to be correctly interpreted when parsing and stringifying. For example, an array of user objects might be represented in JSON as javascript

let jsonString = '[{"name": "John," "age":30}, {"name": "Jane," "age":25}]';

let users = JSON.parse(jsonString); users.forEach(user => console.log(user.name));

This code parses the JSON string into an array of JavaScript objects and then iterates over the array, logging each user's name. Understanding how to work with these data types ensures developers can effectively manipulate and use JSON data within their applications.

Error handling is another crucial aspect of working with JSON. Parsing invalid JSON strings with `JSON.parse()` will throw a syntax error, which must be caught and handled gracefully. This can be done using a try-catch block: javascript let jsonString = '{"name": "John," "age":30'; // Invalid JSON try { let user = JSON.parse(jsonString); console.log(user);

} catch (error) { console.error('Failed to parse JSON:', error);}

In this example, the missing closing brace in the JSON string causes `JSON.parse()` to throw an error, which is caught and logged to the console. Proper error handling ensures that applications remain robust and user-friendly even when encountering malformed JSON data.

Advanced use cases of JSON parsing and stringifying include custom serialization and deserialization. The `JSON.stringify()` method can take an optional second argument, a replacer function, that controls how object values are stringified. Similarly, `JSON.parse()` can take a second argument, a reviver function, to transform values during parsing. For example, to serialize only specific properties of an object, a replacer function might be used: javascript let user = { name: "John", age: 30, password: "secret" }; let jsonString = JSON.stringify(user, (key, value) => { if (key === 'password') { return undefined; // Exclude password from JSON} return value.

}); console.log(jsonString); // Outputs: {"name": "John," "age":30}

In this case, the replacer function omits the `password` property from the JSON string, enhancing security by excluding sensitive information.

Conversely, a reviver function can transform values during parsing. For instance, to convert date strings into JavaScript Date objects, javascript

let jsonString = '{"name":"John", "birthdate":"2000-01-01T00:00:00Z"}';

let user = JSON.parse(jsonString, (key, value) => { if (key === 'birthdate') {

return new Date(value);} return value;}).

console.log(user.birthdate instance of Date); // Outputs: true

Here, the reviver function checks if the key is `birthdate` and, if so, converts the value into a Date object. This allows for more complex data transformations and ensures that parsed JSON data is in the desired format.

In conclusion, parsing JSON data and converting between JSON and JavaScript objects is critical in web development. It allows for efficient data exchange, manipulation of complex data structures, and integration with APIs. By mastering methods like `JSON.parse()` and `JSON.stringify(),` developers can seamlessly convert data between JSON and JavaScript objects, handle various data types, manage nested structures, and ensure robust error handling. Advanced techniques like custom serialization and deserialization further enhance the flexibility and power of working with JSON, making it an indispensable tool in the modern developer's toolkit. Understanding and leveraging these capabilities allows for creating dynamic, data-driven web applications that are both efficient and maintainable.

CHAPTER X

Debugging and Testing

Debugging JavaScript

Web developers need to be proficient in JavaScript debugging to find and correct bugs in their code and ensure that web apps function correctly. Because JavaScript is a dynamic language with loose typing, it frequently results in several common mistakes. Debugging with browser developer tools and understanding how to identify and fix these mistakes can significantly expedite development and enhance the quality of the code.

In JavaScript, "undefined is not a function" is one of the most common mistakes. This happens when the code tries to call something that isn't specified as a function. Typographical errors, including mispronouncing a function name or attempting to invoke a method on an undefined object, frequently cause this error. Developers should first confirm that the function or process they are trying to call is spelled correctly and exists before trying to remedy this. This error can also be avoided by making sure the object on which the method is called is declared.

The "null or undefined reference" error is another often occurring mistake that arises when the code attempts to access a property or method on an object that is either null or undefined. This usually happens when asynchronous actions fail to return the anticipated data or when variables are not initialized correctly. To fix this, developers should use conditional statements to determine whether the object is null or undefined before accessing an object's attributes or methods. By securely accessing nested properties, tools like optional chaining (e.g., {object?. Property}) in contemporary JavaScript can also assist in reducing this problem.

Another common problem in JavaScript is syntax mistakes, which are typically brought on by misplaced or absent characters like braces, semicolons, and commas. The browser's JavaScript engine normally highlights these mistakes, making finding and rectifying them simple. Syntax errors can be avoided by carefully checking the code for typos or missing characters and using a linter. Syntax errors are less likely to occur since liners like ESLint enforce coding standards and offer real-time feedback on syntax problems.

When an operation is carried out on a value of an incompatible type, type errors arise. Type errors can occur, for example, when attempting to manipulate a number using the string method or when arithmetic is applied to a non-numeric item. Before performing any operations on variables, developers should ensure they are of the expected type to fix type errors. Correct data type management can be aided by the use of explicit type conversions (such as {Number(string Value)}). Furthermore, robust typing can be enforced, and type errors can be caught at build time using TypeScript, a superset of JavaScript.

Errors about scope, like "variable is not defined" or "variable is not accessible," arise when variables are either not stated correctly or are obscured by other variables. Because of JavaScript's function scope and block scope (first introduced with ES6's `let` and `const`), variable accessibility can occasionally be unclear. Developers should know the distinction between function scope and block scope and when to define variables using `let` and `const` to prevent scope-related issues. Excessive use of closures and steering clear of global variables complicate scope management.

Debugging JavaScript requires the use of browser developer tools, which are standard. The robust developer tools that come with modern browsers like Chrome, Firefox, and Edge offer a variety of functions for code inspection and debugging. Since the Console tab logs JavaScript errors, warnings, and custom messages, it's frequently the first place to look for faults. Developers can rapidly spot problems and learn possible causes by reviewing the console output.

Developers can see and debug their code via the Browser Developer Tools' Sources tab. Developers can establish breakpoints, step through code execution, and examine variable values using the code editor interface it offers. By placing breakpoints on particular lines of code, developers can halt the program's execution at precise places, allowing them to inspect the application's current state and pinpoint potential trouble spots. Step-by-step execution (step over, step into, and step out) facilitates comprehension of the interplay between various code segments and the code flow.

For debugging problems with HTTP requests and responses, the Network tab is helpful. It displays comprehensive details about every network request, such as headers, status codes, and response data. By examining network traffic, developers can identify problems like unsuccessful requests, inaccurate response data, or sluggish load times. This is very useful for loading external resources or interacting with APIs.

Developers can view and edit HTML and CSS in real time using the Elements tab, which offers a live view of the Document Object Model. Debugging layout, stylistic, and element property issues can benefit from this. Without changing the source code directly, developers may experiment with alternative styles and properties by changing the Elements tab, which is instantly reflected in the browser.

Tools for controlling client-side data storage, including cookies, local storage, and session storage, are available under the Application tab. Debugging problems about user sessions, data persistence, and state management requires this. Developers can check if their application is correctly saving and retrieving information by viewing and changing stored data.

The Performance tab records and displays a variety of metrics, including CPU, memory, and rendering timings, to assist developers in analyzing the performance of their web applications. Developers can optimize their code and improve the application's responsiveness by locating performance bottlenecks. This involves identifying problems such as lingering scripts, overuse of DOM manipulation, and ineffective animations.

Finally, memory leaks and optimal memory utilization are addressed using the Memory tab. It offers capabilities for tracking memory allocation, identifying detached DOM nodes, and taking memory snapshots. Developers may guarantee that their program stays effective and does not utilize excessive resources by monitoring memory consumption, which will improve user experience.

Debugging JavaScript entails identifying and resolving typical mistakes, including null references, undefined functions, syntax errors, type errors, and scope-related problems. A crucial component of this procedure is using browser developer tools, which offer an extensive feature set for code inspection, debugging, and optimization. Developers can improve their debugging skills through efficient use of these tools, resulting in more reliable and efficient online apps. By knowing how to use and navigate each tab in the developer tools, developers can detect and fix problems more quickly, which enhances the quality and dependability of their work.

Testing JavaScript Code

Testing JavaScript code is critical in modern web development, ensuring that applications function correctly, are reliable, and maintain a high-quality standard. It helps developers identify and fix bugs early, verify that their code behaves as expected, and provide a safety net for future changes. The importance of testing cannot be overstated, as it directly impacts software's stability, performance, and maintainability.

One of the primary reasons for testing JavaScript code is to catch bugs early in the development process. By writing tests, developers can immediately detect issues that might otherwise go unnoticed until later stages, where they are typically more costly and time-consuming to fix. Early bug detection allows for quicker resolution and reduces the likelihood of bugs affecting end-users. This proactive approach to quality assurance is essential for delivering reliable and robust applications.

Testing also serves as documentation for the codebase. Well-written tests describe the intended behavior of the code, providing a clear and concise reference for how different parts of the application are supposed to work. This is particularly useful for new developers joining a project or revisiting code after a long period. Tests can demonstrate edge cases, expected inputs and outputs, and how different components interact, enhancing the codebase's overall understanding.

Moreover, testing fosters a sense of confidence in the code. When developers know that tests cover their code, they can make changes and refactor with the assurance that if something breaks, the tests will catch it. This confidence is crucial for maintaining and evolving a codebase over time, as it allows for more aggressive optimization and improvement efforts without the fear of introducing new bugs.

Testing frameworks are indispensable tools for implementing tests in JavaScript. They provide the structure, utilities, and conventions to write and execute tests effectively. Two of the most popular JavaScript testing frameworks are Jest and Mocha, each with unique features and advantages.

Jest, developed by Facebook, is a comprehensive testing framework that works seamlessly with JavaScript projects, particularly those using React. One of Jest's standout features is its ease of use. It comes with a rich set of features out of the box, including a powerful assertion library, a mocking library, and support for asynchronous tests. Jest's zero-configuration setup means developers can start writing tests immediately without spending time on the initial configuration.

Jest's snapshot testing is another powerful feature, handy for testing UI components. Snapshot tests capture the output of one element at a particular point in time and store it as a snapshot. When the test runs again, Jest compares the current output with the stored snapshot and alerts the developer if there are differences. This makes it easy to detect unintended changes in the UI and ensures that components render correctly.

Additionally, Jest runs tests in parallel, significantly speeding up the testing process, especially in large codebases. Its intelligent test runner prioritizes tests affected by recent changes, further optimizing the test execution time. Jest also provides excellent code coverage reports, highlighting the parts of the codebase that are tested and those that are not, helping developers identify areas that need more thorough testing.

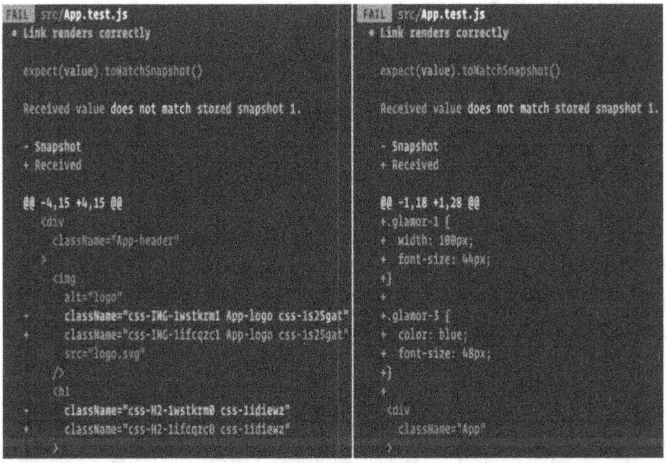

```
FAIL  src/App.test.js
  ● Link renders correctly

    expect(value).toMatchSnapshot()

    Received value does not match stored snapshot 1.

    - Snapshot
    + Received

    @@ -4,15 +4,15 @@
        <div
          className="App-header"
        >
          <img
            alt="logo"
    -       className="css-IMG-1wstkrm1 App-logo css-1s25gat"
    +       className="css-IMG-1ifcqzc1 App-logo css-1s25gat"
            src="logo.svg"
          />
          <h1
    -       className="css-H2-1wstkrm0 css-1idiewz"
    +       className="css-H2-1ifcqzc0 css-1idiewz"
          >
```

```
FAIL  src/App.test.js
  ● Link renders correctly

    expect(value).toMatchSnapshot()

    Received value does not match stored snapshot 1.

    - Snapshot
    + Received

    @@ -1,18 +1,28 @@
    + .glamor-1 {
    +   width: 100px;
    +   font-size: 44px;
    + }
    +
    + .glamor-3 {
    +   color: blue;
    +   font-size: 48px;
    + }
    +
      <div
        className="App"
      >
```

On the other hand, Mocha is a highly flexible and extensible testing framework that provides a solid foundation for writing tests. Unlike Jest, Mocha requires additional libraries for assertions, mocking, and other functionalities, allowing developers to choose their preferred tools. This modularity makes Mocha a versatile choice for various types of projects.

Mocha's flexibility is one of its greatest strengths. It can be configured to run in different environments, including Node.js and the browser, making it suitable for testing server-side and client-side JavaScript. Mocha's simple and expressive syntax allows for precise and readable test definitions, which other developers can easily understand.

To write assertions in Mocha, developers often use libraries like Chai, which provides a variety of assertion styles such as should, expect, and assert. This flexibility allows developers to choose the style best suits their needs and preferences. Chai's extensive range of matches ensures that almost any condition can be tested, from simple value checks to complex deep equality comparisons.

For mocking and spying, developers commonly use Sinon with Mocha. Sinon provides powerful tools for creating test doubles, allowing developers to replace natural objects with mocks, stubs, and spies. This is particularly useful for isolating the unit of code being tested and verifying interactions with dependencies.

Both Jest and Mocha support asynchronous testing, which is crucial for modern JavaScript applications that frequently interact with APIs, databases, and other asynchronous processes. Asynchronous tests can be written using callbacks, promises, or async/await syntax, depending on the developer's preferences and the test's specific requirements.

To illustrate the use of these frameworks, consider a simple function that fetches user data from an API. Here's how one might write tests for this function using Jest:

j"script // fetchUser.js async function fetcher(userId) { const response = await fetch(`https://api.example.com/users/${userId}`); if (!response. ok) {throw new Error('User not found);const user = await response.json(); return user; module.exports = fetch user.

javascrip"// fetchUser.test.js const fetch user = require('./fetchUser')global.fetch = jest.fn(() =>Promise.resolve({ok: true,JSON: () => Promise.resolve({ id: 1, name: 'John Doe' }),test('fetches user data successfully', async () => const user = await fetchUser(1); expect(user).toEqual({ id: 1, name: 'John Doe' }); test('throws an error when user is not found', async () => {

global.fetch = jest.fn(() => Promise.resolve({ ok: false })); await expect(fetchUser(999)).rejects.throw('User not found);});

In this example, Jest's capabilities replace the `fetch` function, allowing the tests to run without making network requests. The first test checks that the function correctly fetches user data, while the second test verifies that an error is thrown when the user is not found.

Using Mocha and Chai, the same tests might look like this: javascript // fetchUser.js async function fetcher(userId) {const response = await fetch(`https://api.example.com/users/${userId}`); if (!response. ok) {throw new Error('User not found); }const user = await response.json(); return user; module.exports = fetch user; javascript // fetchUser.test.js

const chai = require('chai').

const expect = chai.expect.

const fetch user = require('./fetchUser').

const sinon = require('sinon').

global.fetch = require('node-fetch').

Describe('fetchUser', () => { afterEach(() => { Sinon.restore(); }); it('fetches user data successfully', async () => { sinon.stub(global, 'fetch').resolves({ ok: true, json: () => Promise.resolve({ id: 1, name: 'John Doe' }),}); const user = await fetchUser(1); expect(user).to.deep.equal({ id: 1, name: 'John Doe' }); }); it('throws an error when user is not found', async ()

sinon.stub(global, 'fetch').resolves({ ok: false }) await fetchUser(999);} catch (error) {expect(error.message).to.equal('User not found')

This example uses Mocha as the test framework, Chai for assertions, and Sinon for mocking the `fetch` function. The tests serve the same purpose as the Jest example, ensuring the `fetchUser` function behaves correctly under different conditions.

In conclusion, testing JavaScript code is an indispensable practice that ensures application reliability, quality, and maintainability. Testing significantly enhances the development process by catching bugs early, providing clear documentation, and fostering confidence in the code. Testing frameworks like Jest and Mocha offer robust tools and features to write, execute, and manage tests effectively. Jest's ease and powerful built-in features make it an excellent choice for many projects, particularly those using React. Mocha's flexMocha and extensibility, combined with libraries like Chai and Sinon, provide a versatile and powerful testing environment suitable for various applications. By leveraging these frameworks, developers can ensure their JavaScript code is thoroughly tested and robust, ultimately leading to more reliable and high-quality software.

Writing Unit Tests

Writing unit tests is a fundamental practice in software development that ensures individual units or components of a software application work as intended. These tests help identify and fix bugs early in development, contributing to more robust, reliable, and maintainable code. Creating test cases, running them, and interpreting their results are essential skills for developers to master.

Unit testing involves writing test cases covering specific functionality within the code. A unit test typically tests a single function or method, ensuring it performs correctly under various conditions. Test cases should be designed to cover both typical use cases and edge cases, including valid and invalid inputs. This comprehensive approach ensures that the code is tested thoroughly and behaves as expected in different scenarios.

Creating compelling test cases begins with understanding the unit's requirements and behavior. Developers should identify the inputs the unit can receive and the corresponding outputs it should produce. For example, if testing a function that adds two numbers, test cases should include typical values (e.g., positive integers), edge cases (e.g., zero or negative numbers), and invalid inputs (e.g., non-numeric values). By covering various scenarios, developers can ensure that the function handles all possible inputs correctly.

When writing test cases, it is essential to follow best practices to ensure that the tests are clear, maintainable, and effective. Each test case should be independent, meaning that the result of one test should not affect the outcome of another. This independence makes it easier to pinpoint the source of any failures. Additionally, test cases should be small and focused, testing only one aspect of the unit's behavior at a time. This approach makes it easier to understand what each test verifies and simplifies debugging when a test fails.

A good practice is to follow the Arrange-Act-Assert (AAA) pattern when writing test cases. In the Arrange step, developers set up the necessary conditions for the test, such as initializing variables and creating any required objects. In the Act step, they execute the code being tested. Finally, in the Assert step, they verify that the result matches the expected outcome. This structured approach makes test cases more readable and easier to understand.

Once test cases are written, they must be executed to verify that the code behaves as expected. Testing frameworks such as Jest, Mocha, and Jasmine provide tools to run tests and report the results. These frameworks allow developers to organize tests into suites, which can be run together or individually. Running tests frequently during development helps catch issues early and ensures that new changes do not introduce regressions.

Interpreting test results is a critical part of the unit testing process. When all tests pass, it indicates that the code is working as expected for the scenarios covered by the tests. However, when a test fails, developers need to diagnose the cause of the failure and fix the underlying issue. Test frameworks provide detailed reports on which tests failed and why, helping developers quickly identify and address problems.

A common challenge in interpreting test results is dealing with false positives and false negatives. A false positive occurs when a test passes despite the code containing a bug, while a false negative occurs when a test fails even though the code is correct. To minimize false positives, developers should ensure their tests are thorough and cover all relevant scenarios. To reduce false negatives, they should make sure that their tests are correctly set up and that the conditions being tested are accurately defined.

In addition to verifying correctness, unit tests can also help with refactoring code. Refactoring involves making changes to the code's structure without altering its external behavior. Having a comprehensive suite of unit tests provides a safety net during refactoring, as the tests will catch any unintended changes in behavior. This allows developers to improve the code's structure and readability with confidence, knowing that any errors introduced will be quickly identified.

Another benefit of unit testing is that it facilitates continuous integration and continuous deployment (CI/CD) practices. In a CI/CD pipeline, tests are automatically run every time code is committed to the repository. This automated testing helps ensure that the codebase remains stable and that new changes do not introduce bugs. By integrating unit tests into the CI/CD pipeline, developers can catch issues early and maintain high code quality.

To illustrate the process of writing unit tests, consider a simple example of a function that calculates the factorial of a number. The factorial of a non-negative integer \(n \) is the product of all positive integers less than or equal to \(n \). The function should return 1 for an input of 0, as the factorial of 0 is defined as 1. Here is how one might write unit tests for this function using the Jest framework:

First, the factorial function is implemented as follows: javascript factorial.js function factorial(n) if (n < 0) {throw new Error('Negative input not allowed).

if (n === 0) {return 1. return n * factorial(n - 1). module.exports = factorial.

Next, the unit tests for the factorial function are written in a separate file:

javascript factorial.test.js const factorial == require('./factorial'); test('calculates factorial of 0',

expect(factorial(0)).toBe(1)

test('calculates factorial of positive integers', ()

expect(factorial(1)).toBe(1).

expect(factorial(2)).toBe(2).

expect(factorial(3)).toBe(6).

expect(factorial(4)).toBe(24).

expect(factorial(5)).toBe(120)

.

test('throws error for negative input', () => { expect(() => factorial(-1)).throw('Negative input not allowed).

In this example, three test cases are created to verify the factorial function's behavior. The first test checks that the factorial of 0 is 1. The second test verifies the function's correctness for a range of positive integers. The third test ensures that the function throws an error for negative input. These tests cover typical use cases, edge cases, and invalid inputs, providing comprehensive coverage of the factorial function's behavior.

To run these tests, the Jest framework is used. Jest can be run from the command line with a simple command, and it will automatically find and execute the test files, providing a report on the test results. If all tests pass, the output will indicate that the function works correctly for the tested scenarios. If any test fails, Jest will provide detailed information about the failure, including which test failed and why. This information helps developers quickly identify and fix the issue.

Running tests frequently is crucial for maintaining code quality. Developers should run tests after making any changes to the code to ensure that the changes do not introduce new bugs. Automated testing tools can integrate with version control systems to run tests automatically whenever code is committed, providing immediate feedback on the code's quality.

Interpreting test results involves analyzing the output provided by the testing framework. When a test passes, it confirms that the code behaves as expected for the tested scenario. However, when a test fails, developers need to investigate the cause of the failure. The testing framework's output will typically include information about the expected and actual results, which can help identify discrepancies and guide the debugging process.

When a test fails, the first step is to reproduce the issue by rerunning the test and verifying the failure. Next, developers should review the test case and the tested code to understand why the failure occurred. It may be due to a bug in the code, an incorrect assumption in the test, or an issue with the test setup. Once the cause is identified, developers can make the necessary changes to fix the problem and rerun the tests to verify the fix.

In conclusion, writing unit tests is a vital practice for ensuring the quality and reliability of software. Developers can verify that their code behaves as expected by creating comprehensive test cases that cover a wide range of scenarios. Running tests frequently help catch issues early and provides confidence in the code's correctness. Interpreting test results involves analyzing the output from the testing framework to identify and fix any problems. Using best practices such as the AAA pattern, keeping tests independent and focused, and integrating tests into a CI/CD pipeline can significantly enhance the effectiveness of unit testing. Mastering these skills enables developers to produce robust, reliable, and maintainable software that meets high-quality standards.

CONCLUSION

Excellent for finishing "JavaScript for Beginners: Unlocking the Power of Web Development: A Comprehensive Guide to Mastering JavaScript from Scratch." You have gained a strong foundation in JavaScript by working through these chapters, covering everything from the language's fundamentals to more complex subjects like asynchronous programming and API integration.

As you've progressed through this book, you've not only gained theoretical knowledge but also practical skills that are essential for any aspiring web developer. You've learned to set up your development environment, manipulate the DOM, handle events, and debug and test your code. These skills are not just for the book, but they are the tools that will prove invaluable in your real-world projects. You've also gained insight into best practices and the importance of writing clean, efficient code.

Your newfound knowledge equips you to create dynamic and interactive web applications. But remember, the key to mastering JavaScript, like any other skill, is not just practice but consistent practice and continuous learning. The world of web development is constantly evolving, and staying abreast of the latest trends and technologies will ensure your skills remain sharp and relevant.

As you progress, don't hesitate to experiment with new ideas and build your projects—the challenges you encounter, and the solutions you devise will deepen your understanding and enhance your proficiency.

Thank you for buying and reading/listening to our book. If you found this book useful/helpful please take a few minutes and leave a review on the platform where you purchased our book. Your feedback matters greatly to us.